CHRISTMAS IN DENMARK

Raadhuspladsen—*town hall square*—*Copenhagen*

CHRISTMAS IN DENMARK

CHRISTMAS AROUND THE WORLD FROM WORLD BOOK

World Book Encyclopedia, Inc.
a Scott Fetzer company
Chicago

STAFF

Publisher
William H. Nault

Editorial

Editor in chief
Robert O. Zeleny

Executive editor
Dominic J. Miccolis

Associate editor
Maureen M. Mostyn

Senior editor
Scott Thomas

Rights and permissions
Janet T. Peterson

Writer
Terry Fertig

Art

Executive art director
William Hammond

Art director
Roberta Dimmer

Assistant art director
Joe W. Gound

Designer
Strizek & Associates

Crafts artist
Valerie Nelson

Photography director
John S. Marshall

Photographs editor
Sandra Ozanick

Illustrators
Rick Incrocci
Roberta Polfus

Product production

Executive director
Peter Mollman

Manufacturing
Joseph C. La Count

Research and development
Henry Koval

Pre-press services
Jerry Stack, Director
Janice M. Rossing
Alfred J. Mozdzen

The editors wish to thank the many people who took part in the development of this book. Special appreciation goes to Margit Kjeldbjerg, Jenny Jensen, Linda Steffensen, Elsa Steffensen, Chris Steffensen, Ida Sloth Bonnevie, Biba Roesch, Claus Dyrlund, Louise Virgin, Hugo Petersen of the Danish Consulate General, Chicago, and the staff of *The Danish Pioneer*, Hoffman Estates, Illinois.

ISBN 0-7166-0886-3
Library of Congress Catalog Card No. 86–50556
a/hf

CONTENTS

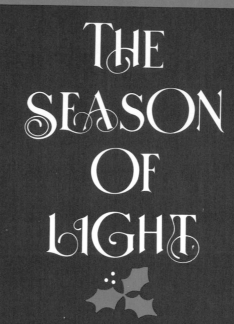

THE
SEASON
OF
LIGHT

Copenhagen, the capital of Denmark, has been called the Paris of the north. The comparison between these two great cities may be unnecessary, for Copenhagen is unique and certainly has an identity all its own. But the comparison is, in some ways, apt. Like Paris, Copenhagen is a sophisticated, gay, fun-loving place, and like Paris, it is a city of light. In the summer months, it is alive with the light of the innumerable twinkling bulbs that decorate the beloved Tivoli Gardens in the center of the city, and in the summer months, all of Copenhagen basks in the clear, warm light of the sun. On the longest day of the year, the summer solstice, the citizens of Denmark enjoy a full 18 hours of sunlight.

But Copenhagen is, as the comparison with Paris notes, a city of the north. In the winter months, the lights of Tivoli are turned off, and the days are short, very short. Like Moscow, Copenhagen receives slightly less than six hours of sunlight on the winter solstice, December 21. But unlike Moscow, Copenhagen is never plunged into gloom and darkness. It remains as gay and fun-loving on the shortest day of the year as it is on the longest. And even in the depths of winter, Copenhagen remains a city of light. The winter solstice falls within *Jul*, the Danish Christmas season, and there are few places in the world where Christmas is celebrated with such joy and relish and with such a burst of light. To dispel the gloom of the pervasive twilight, the

Danes light candles, thousands upon thousands of candles. In fact, the Danes burn so many candles that the nation consumes more candles per capita than any other country on earth.

In Denmark, lighted Christmas candles appear everywhere: in homes, schools, and, of course, in churches. It is not unusual to see a candle burning at midday on a busy office desk or on a workbench at a bustling factory. In Denmark, the workplace is an extension of the home and, as such, is an appropriate location for yet another candle. In America, a lighted candle on a desk would probably be considered slightly odd if not a distinct fire hazard. But in Denmark, the practice of lighting a candle to push back the dark, to introduce a little *hyggelig* (HOO guh lee), an atmosphere of warmth and coziness, is a very old tradition, a tradition much older than Christmas.

Long before Harald Bluetooth introduced Christianity to his Viking subjects, the people of the

In Denmark, a profusion of candles are lighted to dispel the gloom of the long winter nights before Jul.

north celebrated *Jul* with the setting of great fires. *Jul,* a word absorbed into English as *Yule,* was probably initiated into the language by Vikings, who raided and, eventually, settled on the English coastline. The word is believed to derive from a much older word, *hjul,* which means wheel, and refers to the winter solstice and the "turning" of winter into spring and darkness into light. Perhaps the long, cold, dark season of the north produced the fear that the fiery warmth and strength of the sun would never come around again, and winter would, thus, continue forever. *Jul* was celebrated by the pagan Norsemen with a great feast in honor of Odin, the lord of the skies and master of the gods. Lighted candles, torches, and bonfires were a sign of the Viking's devotion as well as a supplication that Odin would command the sun's return as soon as possible.

The celebration of the pre-Christian *Jul* was also a festival of the dead. On the longest, darkest night of the year, the souls of the dead were believed to come home again. The dark was feared and thought to be inhabited by ghosts, witches, goblins, and those giants and dwarfs who possessed evil powers and who played deceitful tricks on the unwary. Tales of old Norse and German mythology, such as Wagner's *Ring of the Nibelung,* are filled with such creatures who wreak havoc for the sport of it. No wonder then, that light—the light of fires, torches, and candles—was a necessary ingredient of the *Jul* celebration.

Christianity supplanted the old religion—Odin, Frey, Thor, and all the ancient gods of Valhalla—in the 900's. Although *Jul* remained *Jul,* it also became Christmas. The old feast of light in honor of Odin became a feast of light in honor of Christ, the "light of the world." The celebration of death became a celebration of birth. The old gods and spirits, thus, slowly disappeared; but not quite.

One of the old spirits has refused to give up *Jul.* After the proliferation of candles, the next surest sign of the coming of Christmas to Denmark is the appearance of *nisser,* which is the plural of *nisse.* A *nisse* can be described, but is somewhat harder to define. A *nisse* is always a he, and he is short, like one of the ancient dwarfs, but is usually less troublesome than those dwarfs who connived with and against the gods. *Nisser* wear homespun clothes—breeches and a smock of unbleached wool—and a red cap; they sport long, gray beards, which makes them sound a little like Santa Claus. Like Santa, they are very much a part of the Christmas season, and like Santa, they are plagued by dozens of impostors who show up everywhere—in department stores, on street corners, in store windows, on television—purporting to be the genuine article. But Danes know a *nisse* when they see one, just as Americans know their Santa. Like old Saint Nick, a *nisse* is very clever about getting around without actually being seen, and also like Santa, a *nisse* expects a

snack on Christmas Eve. But beyond these token similarities, *nisser* and Santa Claus are not really much alike.

A *nisse* doesn't really do much, and he most certainly doesn't go in for anything as strenuous as delivering gifts. He is rather more gruff than jolly, and he much prefers an attic or hayloft to a sooty chimney stack. Danish children, of course, love their *nisser,* but *nisser* have no great affinity for children over adults. If Santa is not remembered with a plate of cookies on Christmas Eve, he is not really peeved, but a *nisse* who is not fed his porridge on Christmas Eve can be cantankerous, if not downright dangerous. No one knows just how dangerous because no Dane would risk the consequences of such an insult. Santa's good behavior can, of course, be taken for granted; he is, after all, a saint. Everyone in Denmark knows that a *nisse* is no saint.

While everyone agrees on a *nisse's* lack of saintliness, even experts cannot agree on what, exactly, a *nisse* is. Some consider him a sprite, that is, an elf, or a fairy, or a goblin. In the countryside, he is thought of as a spirit of one's forefathers who, during *Jul,* comes round to check that the family farm or the ancestral home is being cared for in the proper manner. Scholars insist that *nisser*

Lavish window displays tempt Copenhagen shoppers with an amazing variety of Christmas treats, decorations, and, of course, candles. Danes use more candles, per capita, than any other people on earth.

are related to the devil. The word *nis* is identical to *Niels,* and in Denmark the devil is referred to as Old Niels, much as the devil in England is called Old Nick. Although *nisser* are known to hang about with cats who, nonbelievers insist, actually consume that Christmas porridge, no self-respecting Dane really considers a *nisse* a devil. It is true he is mischievous, but he is certainly not downright evil.

Now there are a few hard facts about *nisser:* they are small; they are mischievous; they are old, very old; some say they are old enough to be acquainted with Odin and the other gods of Valhalla, and that, of course, is very old. *Nisser* have always hung around during *Jul.* And there is no reason to think that won't continue in the future. It is well known that the *nisser* prefer the dark, which is one reason they may appear only during the long nights of December. It has been suggested that a *nisse* might be a little less elusive if there were not so many candles putting out so much light. It has also been suggested that there might be fewer candles burning if there were not so many *nisser* lurking. It's a bit of a stand-off, and one that is not likely to be resolved quickly, for the Danes like *Jul* just the way it is. They like their *nisser,* of course, but they also like their candles. Both appear simultaneously around Advent, which, appropriately, means "the coming." The coming, of course, refers to the coming of Christ. But in Denmark, it also points to the

Above: **Nisser,** *or Christmas sprites, have been part of the Danish* Jul *since pre-Christian times. These two, well over one hundred years old, are in the form of* pantins, *or cardboard jumping jacks, a Christmas toy popular in Denmark for over two centuries.*

Right: A nisse *doll, complete with Christmas Eve porridge. Modern* nisser *are more elf- or gnome-like in appearance than their nineteenth-century ancestors.*

That long wait for **Juleaften**, *or Christmas Eve, is nearly over when the fourth candle, representing the final Sunday before Christmas, is lighted on the Advent wreath.*

coming of *Jul* and everything that implies.

In Danish churches, Advent, the fourth Sunday before Christmas, is celebrated with special services. In Danish homes, Advent is celebrated with the arrival of the season's first decoration: a beautiful Advent wreath of evergreen boughs that harbors four tall, slender white or red candles. The wreath is hung above or set on the dining room table. On the first Sunday before Christmas, one candle is lit, and the most festive and celebrated season of the year is launched. On the second Sunday of Advent, the first candle on the wreath and an additional candle are lit. The ritual continues

Sunday after Sunday until, on the last Sunday before Christmas, all four candles are lit together and the realization that Christmas Eve is about to arrive is apparent in the eyes and on the glowing candlelit faces of all those gathered around the table—young and old alike.

The Danes have also devised another method for burning away the days before Christmas—calendar candles. Children often begin the countdown on December 1 by lighting this tall candle with 24 evenly spaced markings, one for each day until Christmas. The candle is allowed to burn only down to the next mark, at which point it is promptly extinguished. The chil-

dren must wait until the next evening to light the candle again. And so it goes each night until Christmas. But as the candle gets shorter, so does the wait.

The first of December is also the date on which most Danish families, to the delight of the children, put out their Christmas or Advent calendars, which range from the very simple to the quite elaborate. Each day before Christmas one of the 24 numbered doors or windows is opened to reveal yet another treasured symbol of the holidays: cookies or toys or candles or, of course, *nisser*. The store-bought variety of calendars are, naturally, replaced every year. Many Danish families, however, make their own Advent calendar. These often include hooks instead of windows. From each hook, a tiny package is hung, and on each of the 24 days before Christmas, a new package is unwrapped. The tiny packages contain small gifts—a toy car or a tiny doll or a package of gum or a wrapped chocolate. The gifts are not lavish, but the daily ceremony of unwrapping another gift makes the endless wait until Christmas bearable, as well as fun.

In years past, during hard times, Danish families improvised Christmas calendars using a potato and wooden matchsticks. The potato was made to resemble a pig. Hogs are an important farming commodity in Denmark. At one time, it was said, the hogs of Denmark outnumbered the people by two to one. And so pigs often appear as a favored symbol, even at Christmas. Wooden matchsticks were placed in the potato pig. Each day, a matchstick was pulled out to symbolize the counting off of the days before Christmas.

In Denmark, Christmas calendars often appear in school classrooms. Some teachers allow each member of the class to bring a small, wrapped package to school late in November. These gifts are attached to the calendar, and beginning on the first of December, one or two children a day open a package from the calendar.

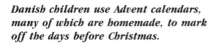
Danish children use Advent calendars, many of which are homemade, to mark off the days before Christmas.

The teacher, of course, makes certain that there are enough presents to go around and that each child has a turn at the calendar.

During *Jul*, children often try to keep their teachers occupied so that homework will not be assigned, and generally, teachers oblige. Christmas in Denmark is not, after all, simply for children. At this time of year, teachers, like everyone else, are preoccupied with holiday plans and thoughts of Christmas. So at this time of year, students are often kept busy learning and singing traditional Christmas hymns and carols or making ornaments and decorations for the home and school. Schoolchildren are also often responsible for making the ornaments with which the town Christmas tree is decorated. Each classroom also has its own real tree to decorate and enjoy.

The *Jul* activities in Danish schools culminate on the day the holiday recess begins. Each class may have its own small celebration with the students and teacher gathered around the classroom tree singing. Treats are shared, and afterwards, all the classes gather in a large room where the school tree is on display. The entire school joins in singing more Christmas songs. A traditional Christmas story, perhaps by Hans Christian Andersen, may be read by the principal. These activities may include an appearance by the *Julemand*, who is a cross between the German *Weihnachtsmann*, the English Father Christmas, and the American Santa Claus.

School Christmas programs often include a visit by the Julemand, *a Danish figure similar to the American Santa Claus.*

Although pre-Christmas activities are great fun, there is also much work to be done in the weeks preceding Christmas. Many preparations must be made. Most Danes agree, however, that preparing for Christmas is never really work.

Throughout Denmark, family members join together to give the house and yard a thorough cleaning. The work begins early in December. Curtains are cleaned. Windows are washed. Floors are scrubbed. The good dishes are washed in anticipation of dinner on Christmas Eve, and the silver and brass are polished. In the country, even the barnyard and stable are not forgotten. It is a very old custom in Denmark to give farm animals and even the birds special attention during the *Jul* season. A sheaf of grain is hung out for the birds, and farm animals are given extra rations of

Polishing the silver in anticipation of Christmas dinner is only a small part of the Jul *housecleaning, a project that involves the entire family.*

food on Christmas Eve. It was once held that a farmer who neglected his animals during *Jul* would have a disastrous year ahead. Although Danes may no longer carry out their tasks with the same fervor with which their ancestors cleaned, most readily admit the necessity of a tidy home during the holidays. One never knows when friends and relatives may drop by for some holiday cheer.

The sharing of holiday cheer with friends and neighbors is an essential part of the Christmas season in Denmark, and nothing is more important than having freshly baked Christmas goodies—cookies, cakes, and pastry—for callers to sample. Never would a host or hostess think of sending a visitor away during the *Jul* season without a taste of the family's

good cheer. In Denmark, it is a very old belief that a visitor who leaves the house without being fed may carry away the Christmas spirit. Thus, every Danish kitchen buzzes with activity and is filled with the aroma of sweets and spices in the weeks before Christmas.

Very early in December, the dough must be mixed for *brune kager* or brown Christmas cookies; the dough can, thus, sit in the refrigerator for several weeks, which allows time for it to ripen and the flavors to meld. These cookies are a mixture of brown sugar, assorted spices, orange rind, and dark corn syrup, cut into rounds, and topped in the center with half an almond. A second indispensable Danish Christmas cookie is *kleiner*, which are long, narrow cookies made with a luscious butter dough, twisted into a tricky knot, and deep-fried in oil. Both the gingerbread-like *brune kager* and the crisp *kleiner* are a necessity at Christmastime. No Danish household would be without a generous supply of both.

A third Christmas treat, famous throughout Denmark, is *pebbernødder,* or peppernuts. These are small, spice cookies baked very hard—often too hard to eat, in which case they are passed along to the children to use for playing table games. If made properly, however, *pebbernødder* are very tasty and are often included in a bowl filled with nuts, fruits, candies, and marzipan. Marzipan, a rich, almond fondant, is a must during the holiday season. Many families make their own marzipan candies in the shapes of fruits, vegetables, or animals. The pig is, of course, a favorite shape for *Jul.* Beautifully crafted marzipan animals can also be purchased from confectioners' shops, which specialize in the making of this candy during the holiday season.

Other Christmas specialties include *vanillekranse,* or vanilla rings, which are butter cookies shaped into wreaths; *julekage,* or Christmas coffee cake; and Danish kringle, a legendary Danish pastry filled with raisins and almonds. Kringle is, of course, enjoyed by Danes throughout the year.

Danish mothers invite their children to join in and help with the *julebagning,* or Christmas baking, thus passing along the tradition as well as the family recipes. The children's help is also enlisted in the preparation of plates of Christmas baked goods for friends and relatives. In Denmark, no one is allowed to carry away the Christmas spirit, but it is shared generously.

The tradition of giving plates of cookies and pastries has resulted in another *Jul* tradition —the collecting of special Christmas plates—which has spread from Denmark to around the world. Long ago in Europe it was the custom for wealthy families to give plates of sweets and other special foods to their servants at Christmastime. As these plates were finer than any that the serv-

Low on the horizon, the sun casts long, deep shadows across the Danish landscape during the short, precious days of the **Jul** *season.*

In Denmark, guests are always offered a bit of Christmas—cookies, candies, or pastries—for fear they may otherwise steal away the host's Christmas spirit. Baking for **Jul** is a full family project that begins weeks before Christmas.

ants owned, they were treasured and hung on the wall as decoration. Before long the plates became objects of rivalry and were traded and collected passionately. Eventually, more ornate plates began to appear, and the habit of dating them was begun. The porcelain house of Bing and Grøndahl, recognizing this trend, issued, in 1895, the first limited-edition plate to commemorate the holiday season. Entitled "Behind the Frozen Window," the plate pictured Copenhagen's skyline as seen through a frosted window-pane. It is estimated that 500 of these were produced and sold for fifty cents. When Harald Bing ordered his workmen to destroy the mold for the first plate, thus establishing the first known limited-edition collector's plate, little did anyone realize that a new custom was being established. Nor was it realized how valuable a keepsake one of these plates would become; only 13 "Behind the Frozen Window" plates are known to still exist.

In 1908, Royal Copenhagen, Denmark's oldest porcelain maker, followed Bing and Grøndahl's example by producing its own series of Christmas plates. Like the Bing and Grøndahl plates, these were also of the blue and white variety with the date and occasion of issuance fired permanently into the porcelain glaze. The blue and white colors of these keepsakes are appropriate symbols of the season—white for purity and blue for heaven and the Virgin Mary. Both firms use one of the most difficult ceramic techniques, that

For over 90 years, Juleaften plates have pictured Christmas in Denmark to the world. The 1911 Royal Copenhagen plate (top) depicts a sheaf of grain hung out for the birds, an ancient Danish Jul custom. The 1944 Bing and Grøndahl plate (bottom) was intended as a message to the world as well as to the citizens of Denmark. The plate pictures Sorgenfri Castle, where King Christian X was held prisoner by the Nazis for refusing to cooperate with German forces occupying Denmark. Christian X helped facilitate the escape of nearly all Danish Jews to neutral Sweden.

of underglaze painting. After the artist paints the scene, the plate is dipped in glaze, completely obscuring the decoration. When the plate is fired in the kiln, the scene reappears. A design for a Christmas plate may be submitted by any employee of the porcelain house. On Christmas Eve the mold for that year is broken, never to be reproduced.

Through the years, the Christmas plates have told the story of

Denmark and offered to the world a glimpse of the customs and traditions of the Danish *Jul.* While most designs have been simple and charming, a few have been very serious. The 1944 design, for example, protested the Nazi occupation of Denmark by showing the "Sorgenfri" Castle, where King Christian X, who refused to cooperate with the enemy, was held prisoner by the Germans.

A second Danish Christmas

tradition bestowed upon the rest of the world is the use of the familiar Christmas seal on holiday cards and packages. The origin of the first Christmas seal dates back to 1903 when a Danish postal clerk, Einar Holboell, conceived of the idea while sorting large piles of Christmas mail one stormy December evening in Copenhagen. After catching a glimpse through the window of two waifs in the storm, he was saddened by the thought of the many children who suffered from tuberculosis. Suddenly it became very clear to him: Why not produce a decorative stamp which could be placed on letters and parcels during the holidays—and sell it for only a penny? Think of the money that could be raised for the construction of much-needed hospitals for the unfortunate children stricken with this dread disease. Einar Holboell decided it was a wonderful

idea. Fortunately, other prominent citizens agreed and were just as enthusiastic, including the reigning king, Christian IX, who suggested the first stamp bear the likeness of his wife Queen Louise as a sign of support and endorsement. And so the following Christmas, in 1904, the first Christmas seals went on sale in Denmark. Over four million were sold that year, raising $18,000, an amazing achievement at a time when fund drives were unknown.

Norway and Sweden were the first to follow Denmark's lead in this valiant Christmas effort and found their citizens just as willing to contribute to such a worthy cause. In 1907, the idea crossed the ocean to America. Jacob Riis, the noted Danish immigrant and New York social worker and journalist, was instrumental in introducing Americans to Einar Holboell's plan. He had good rea-

son, for six of his brothers had died of tuberculosis. The campaign won the support of the Red Cross and, in 1910, was taken over by the National Tuberculosis Association. Today, over 3,000 organizations are affiliated with the National Tuberculosis Association. TB has also dropped from first to twenty-second place as a cause of death in America.

Today, most Danes continue to send out their Christmas cards and packages smothered with Christmas seals. Each year in Denmark, a new Christmas seal design, usually a work of art, is issued. One of the loveliest blocks of Christmas seals was designed a number of years ago by Queen Margrethe. It featured a sheet of 50 stamps with a design depicting a castle full of music-making angels. Each stamp contributed one small part to the total scene.

Einar Holboell died in 1927.

The issuing of Christmas seals to raise money to fight disease began in Denmark in 1903. This plate of stamps, designed in 1970 by Queen Margrethe II, pictures angels decorating Himmelborgen, *a Danish word loosely translated as the Castle in the Sky or the City of Heaven.*

Danish Christmas cards often picture national symbols of the season—candles, nisser, *and hearts. Rarely opened upon arrival, Christmas cards are saved until* Juleaften *and then opened and passed around the family circle.*

That Christmas his portrait appeared on the Danish Christmas seal of the year, a well deserved honor. He had lived to see his monumental idea travel around the world. Today, 45 countries have adopted the Christmas seal campaign.

During the month of December, the Danish postal service is flooded with more than just the usual heavy load of holiday cards and packages. Thousands of letters addressed to Santa Claus arrive in Copenhagen each year. Danish children do not usually write to Santa. In Denmark, it is not much of a secret that the *Julemand* is actually Poppa. The letters to Santa are written by American children and are addressed to Greenland, the nearest land mass to the North Pole. Although Green-

land, the largest island in the world, lies 1,300 miles from Denmark, it is a Danish province. The letters are, thus, delivered to Copenhagen, and throughout December, kindly ladies volunteer to answer each of these letters so that young writers will not be disappointed and have their Christmas spirit carried off. As a special message from Santa, each reply includes a copy of a short Christmas tale by Hans Christian Andersen, the beloved Danish writer whose work is filled with that special light that is *Jul.*

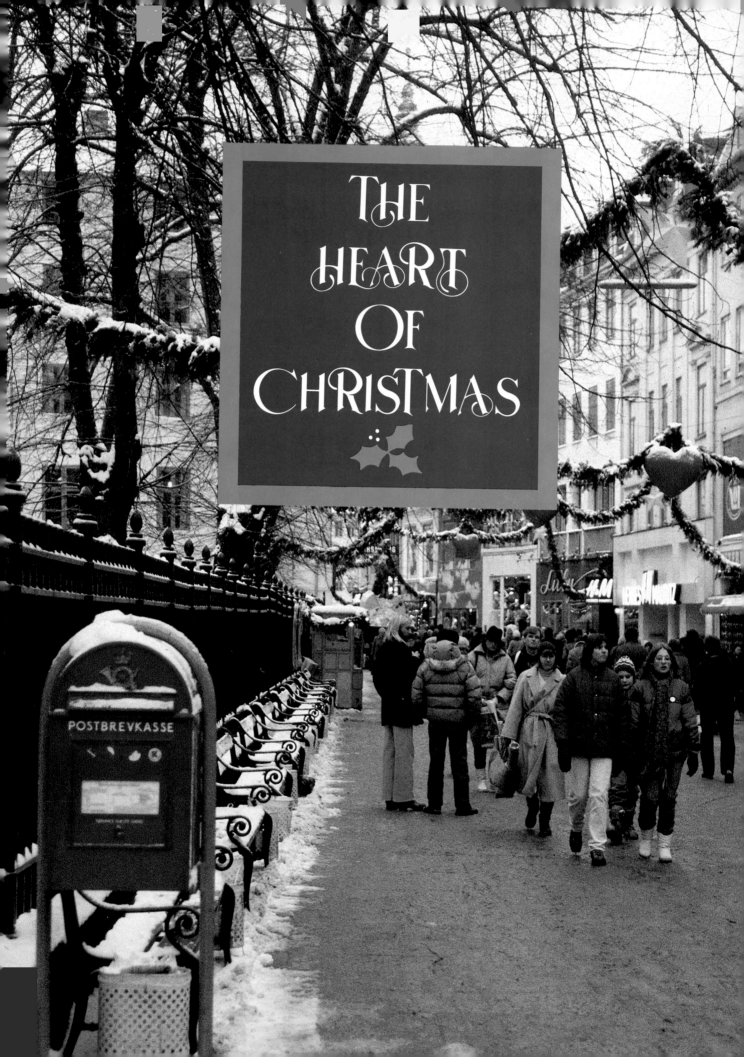

THE
HEART
OF
CHRISTMAS

elebrating a Danish Christmas is no small chore. Preparing for a Christmas with all the traditional trimmings includes decorating the house from cellar to dome. So early in December, all the treasured decorations, which have been packed away for a year, are carefully unwrapped and repositioned in exactly the correct spot. Danes everywhere bedeck their homes at Christmastime with great enthusiasm and dedication. There are brightly colored paper chains, Christmas mobiles, wallhangings, flags, and garlands of every design. And everywhere, there are *julenisser.* The sprites in their long red caps, long white beards, gray breeches, and wooden clogs hang from the curtains and from chandeliers, peek above picture frames, poke from behind mirrors, and stand on windowsills.

Evergreen boughs, mistletoe, and holly, which the Danes call *Kristdorn,* or Christ thorn, are purchased from flower stalls or collected from nearby woods. Most Danish families use pine cones and fresh evergreen branches, often the lower boughs cut from the Christmas tree, to fashion a candled table centerpiece or a wreath for the wall or door. Beneath a typical centerpiece is an exquisite table runner with hand-embroidered hearts or other Christmas motifs. The smell of fir or spruce combined with the scent of candle wax, thus, greets visitors as they cross the threshold of a Danish home during the holiday season.

Danish children, of course, anxiously await the first of December when Mother brings the box of handmade Christmas tree ornaments down from the attic. The children carefully take stock of all the cherished decorations and then mend and fix any broken parts. Once the children are confident that everything is in good repair, Mother puts the box back in its special place until the tree is ready to be decorated.

The traditional Danish Christmas tree always includes many homemade ornaments. If new tree decorations need to be made, and they always do, the whole family participates in its annual "cut and paste day." This is a project that Danes eagerly anticipate during the Advent season. Around mid-December, the family gathers around the dining room table for

Luminaries, votive candles, and strings of electrified candles brighten Denmark's long, winter nights during the season of Jul.

an afternoon of cutting and pasting. Friends are often invited to join the family, and everyone brings scissors, glue, colored paper, and a variety of other materials necessary for producing new ornaments. The older generation fondly recalls when the glue used on "cut and paste day" was made of flour and water and mixed up by Mother.

Naturally, everyone around the table knows that sooner or later there will be a break for something special to eat. Perhaps Mother made *aebleskiver,* delicious, deep-fried, pancake balls, which are a Danish favorite all year long. A tray of the Christmas cookies, which Mother and the children have been busy preparing, may also be set out for all to sample.

But then it's back to the table, where the beautiful ornaments are beginning to take shape. The older family members at the table help the younger ones with just the right method of cutting, folding, and pasting all the traditional specialties for the tree. Hearts are a particular favorite and are everywhere at Christmas—on the table, on mobiles, but especially on the tree. The woven heart baskets that are so characteristic of a Danish Christmas tree are made of glossy red and white paper and can be very basic in design or elaborately woven, depending on the age and abilities of the craftsman. Besides being traditional Christmas colors, red and white are Denmark's national colors; these two colors, thus, predominate the *Jul* season. Denmark's red and white flag, the

On "cut and paste" day, which is nearly a universal event in Denmark, the entire family joins together to repair old decorations and make new ones for the Juletrae, *or Christmas tree.*

Dannebrog, is displayed on all national holidays, and Christmas is no exception. Danes are a patriotic people, and most are proud to display a small Danish flag somewhere in their homes every day of the year. Most Danes, thus, entwine long garlands of miniature Danish flags around the boughs of their Christmas tree.

Paper cones, or cornucopia, are another Christmas ornament common to most Danish Christmas trees. These are usually made from a square of shiny gold or silver paper rolled and pasted into a conical shape. Striped papers are used to give a spiral effect to the cone. When ready to be hung on the tree, the cones, and occasionally the woven hearts, are filled with candies and nuts—a

Christmas Eve treat for the children similar to the candy canes and oranges American children find in their Christmas stockings.

Other typical Danish Christmas tree ornaments include three-dimensional stars made from strips of sparkly white paper elaborately woven into the desired shape. One might also spy a little *nisse* made of red yarn with braided arms and legs hanging from a branch of the Christmas tree. Little drums, bells, wooden figures, and pine cone ornaments are also popular. Festive, brightly colored "poppers" or "crackers," noisemakers that pop when both ends are pulled, are often hung on the tree. Miniature "sparklers," like those Americans burn on the Fourth of July, are another favorite; these are attached to the tree and lighted, like candles, on Christmas Eve. An ornamented star tops nearly every Christmas tree in Denmark.

Christmas trees are a relatively recent development in Denmark. The first *Juletrae,* or Christmas tree, appeared in Holsteinsborg on the Danish island of Fyn in 1808. It arrived via Germany, where trees have been a tradition since at least the 1500's. Early in December, Christmas trees appear for sale in flower markets and on street corners in many towns throughout Denmark. As most families do not put up their tree until *lille Juleaften,* or little Christmas Eve, the day before Christmas Eve, Danes generally try to wait as long as possible before purchasing a tree. But gripped with the fear that all the best ones will soon be gone, and certainly prodded by the young ones who can wait no longer, many break down and buy their tree early. There is, of course, a mad rush to pick the perfect tree and carry it home on foot, by car, or very likely on a bicycle. (Bicycles are very popular in Denmark, particularly in Copenhagen where some buses even have a special rack on the back for carrying bicycles.) In the country, Father might go into the woods or into the farm's stand of timber to chop down a tree for the family's parlor. The children enjoy accompanying him and are often allowed to do so if they promise not to bicker about which tree to choose. But the tree must, then, stand out back and wait for the big day when it will be decorated. While many Danish families

Most Danish Christmas decorations are homemade. Hearts, a national favorite, are an expression of love, family warmth, and good will between men.

Beautifully decorated cones, or cornucopias, are filled with candies and nuts and are, traditionally, hung, like ornaments, from the tree. Like the oranges and hard candy found in American Christmas stockings, the sweet-filled cones are passed out on Christmas Eve as part of the family gift exchange.

put up their *Juletrae* on *lille* Juleaften, December 23, others wait until Christmas Eve to erect their tree. This is particularly true in the numerous fishing villages throughout the land, such as Skagen at the northernmost tip of Denmark. There, children run to the harbor and anxiously pace the docks as they wait for their fisherman fathers to return home and put up the tree.

The Christmas tree in Denmark is usually decorated behind locked doors by Mother, Father, or an older brother or sister. The family's small children are not al- lowed to see the decorated tree until the big celebration after Christmas Eve dinner. Naturally, they zealously attempt to peek through the keyhole or a crack in the door for a glimpse of the glorious *Juletrae*. Like shaking a wrapped package for a clue to the contents, it's all part of the fun of Christmas!

The glittering adornments and decorations of Christmas are not limited to the interiors of Danish homes. Recently, Danes have begun to decorate the outside of their houses with electric lights. These are always white, however,

In Danish cities, Christmas trees are, of course, sold by street vendors. In the country, however, many families continue to cut their own Juletrae *from nearby woods.*

The Dannebrog, the Danish national flag, is displayed for all holidays, and Christmas is no exception. Garlands of miniature paper flags are a favorite decoration for the Christmas tree.

never the multicolored variety. And every city, town, and village has its streets and lightposts strung with evergreen garlands and sparkling white lights. Giant papier-mâché hearts hang over the streets, reminding busy shoppers that *Jul* is a season of brotherly love. Salvation Army bell ringers are, of course, a frequent sight on city street corners at Christmastime, ringing their bells and singing carols. And every town has a tall, lighted Christmas tree in the *raadhuspladsen,* or town hall square, for all to enjoy.

In the weeks before Christmas, the streets in most large cities bustle with people. Many are there for the purpose of tending to their annual Christmas shopping. During the month of December, most specialty shops and department stores, even grocery stores, remain open later than their usual five-thirty closing hour.

Other people strolling the streets come to town solely to enjoy the beauty and absorb the gaiety of the season. The stores with their clever Christmas displays are gaily decorated inside and out. Department-store windows are piled high with gift suggestions for the whole family. Always full of those ever-present *julenisser,* shop windows are adorned with paper hearts or stars, a sprig of fir, or perhaps a small white village church sur-

26

In Denmark, public decorations are lavish. An immense tree, decorated with electrified candles and the traditional, "homemade" hearts, stars, and flags, dominates the atrium of a Copenhagen department store.

rounded with soft, fluffy, cottony snow. In the bakery shop window, animals made of delicious marzipan beckon passers-by to enter and purchase some of this confection to take home for the holidays. The butcher decorates his window with the head of a real pig, a shiny red apple clamped tightly in its jaws. And so as not to dismay the friendly *nisse* who keeps a close watch on the homestead, a red stocking cap is placed on the pig's head. A Danish flag is, of course, perched behind each ear.

Restaurants, too, are brightly decorated; they are very busy during the weeks before Christmas catering to the many Christmas lunches that businesses plan for their clients or employees.

Around mid-December youngsters begin begging for a trip into town to see the Christmas finery or to make personal Christmas purchases, but they also wish to visit the *Julemand.* This jolly gentleman, who resembles our Santa Claus, appears in department stores throughout Denmark

at Christmastime. Danish children pledge their good behavior to the *Julemand,* though they know he does not really bring their gifts; it's Papa or Uncle Hans who has that job. Parents finally give in to their youngsters' wishes, and all enjoy an excursion into town to view the beautiful Christmas sights. For just a short while the whole family becomes a part of the special flurry that is Christmas in Denmark.

JUL AFTEN

Christmas Eve in Denmark, *Juleaften*, is the most important day of the holiday season, as well as the most important day of the year. The day that precedes it, *lille Juleaften*, is, however, the busiest. While delicious smells drift through the house as preparations begin for Christmas Eve dinner, the tree is decorated behind parlor doors; the house is given a last-minute tidying; children are dispatched for forgotten ingredients, last-minute purchases, or a final decoration for the tree; the gifts are wrapped, and this is no small thing. Danes take great pride in how presents are wrapped, and there are many packages to be wrapped. The pile beneath the tree is usually high, for most Danes exchange Christmas gifts with all members of their family, as well as with close friends and colleagues.

As Christmas Eve dawns, Danes all across the country wake with nervous anticipation. The children find it difficult to keep their minds attuned to anything but this evening's celebration. Danish housewives are nervous over dinner, for it must be perfect, and Christmas dinner is usually the sole responsibility of mothers. They seldom get help from other family members in preparing this special meal. Early in the day, the table is set with a special Christmas cloth, the family's finest porcelain and silver, and a centerpiece made of fresh greens and red and white candles. It was once a tradition that the Christmas table be set with two tall candles, which stood at either end of the long table. One represented the husband, and the other symbolized the wife. No one dared extinguish these candles, for they foretold death. The one whose candle burned longer, it was said, would outlive the other.

While Mother prepares dinner, the children of the house are busy with chores that are a traditional part of *Juleaften*. A *juleneg*, which is a sheaf of corn, wheat, barley, or oats, is tied to the porch or balcony, hung in a tree, or perched on a spruce pole positioned by the garden gate, near the barn, or on the roof. The more birds that come to feed on this Yuletide supper, the better; it is a portent of good fortune in the year ahead.

Since all nature is glorified at Christmastime, birds are not the sole recipients of this attention.

The streets of Copenhagen are filled on **lille Juleaften,** *December 23, with shoppers running last-minute errands in preparation for Christmas Eve.*

Children make certain that their pets are well cared for on Christmas Eve, and farmers, throughout the country, give animals an extra portion of food with the Christmas toast, "Eat well, keep well; this is Christmas Eve." It is said the animals in the barn stand at midnight in honor of Christ's birth.

As the day wears on, activities become more hectic. Someone is sent to pick up the relatives who spend Christmas Eve with the family. Though *Juleaften* is generally for the immediate family, grandparents or an elderly aunt or uncle, who may otherwise be alone on this evening, are invited to join the family celebration.

At four o'clock in the afternoon, church bells in towns and villages throughout Denmark begin to chime. They herald the start of the true Christmas celebration. All businesses and stores close. All workers and last-minute shoppers scurry home to get ready for church and the evening ahead.

Mother settles the goose carefully in the oven before the family leaves to attend the five o'clock candlelight service at church. All but a very small percentage of the country's population belong to the Evangelical Lutheran Church, the official state church of Denmark. The largest non-Lutheran religious group in Denmark is Roman Catholic. Danish churches are handsomely decorated for Christmas. Many candles burn amid fragrant evergreen garlands and on the tree near the altar. On this night, the churches of Denmark are filled to capacity. In heavily populated parishes, additional early Christmas services are scheduled to accommodate all of the worshipers. The services are generally short. Ministers long ago realized the necessity of scheduling Christmas Eve services around the Christmas dinner. Pastors, delivering the traditional Christmas sermon, are, of course, well aware that hundreds of browning geese are at stake, and they often cut their sermons short. The service ends, as it began, with the congregation joining the choir in singing traditional Christmas hymns.

As the church empties, family members greet their friends and neighbors with a sincere *"Glaedelig Jul"*—Merry Christmas! With luck, as the people begin their journey home, snow will begin to fall. The Danes are very partial to a white Christmas.

If Mother has timed things right, dinner is ready when the family arrives home from church. But before dinner can begin, one final custom must be completed. A bowl of rice porridge is set out for the *julenisse.* It would not do that he be forgotten on this of all nights. And so, before dinner, children all over Denmark hurry to place the bowl of warm porridge in the attic or barn loft, which, of course, are favorite hiding places of *nisser.*

As everyone finds a place around the dinner table, Mother places a lighted candle in the window, completing another ancient custom. This is done as a welcome sign for any strangers who may be passing by, for no one

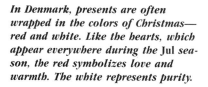

In Denmark, presents are often wrapped in the colors of Christmas— red and white. Like the hearts, which appear everywhere during the Jul *season, the red symbolizes love and warmth. The white represents purity.*

Danish mothers begin dinner early on Christmas Eve. By tradition, the goose must be in the oven before the family sets off for church at dusk.

should go hungry on this night.

The traditional Christmas feast in Denmark begins with *risengrød,* or rice porridge. This is boiled rice mixed with cream and served warm with a sprinkle of cinnamon. Hidden somewhere in the porridge is a whole almond. Whoever finds the almond qualifies for the "almond gift," which is often a piece of marzipan, usually a pig. The lucky one, however, is not to tell of his or her find until everyone has finished their portion of the porridge. Somehow the almond usually ends up on the plate of the youngest member of the family. Very wise mothers often see to it that each of her children finds an almond. Many Danes be-

lieve that *risengrød,* as filling as it is, was specifically served to curb the appetite. In hard times, the food prepared for dinner was not always plentiful enough to satisfy everyone, and the porridge helped to fill one up. In recent years, many Danish families have begun to forgo the rice porridge at the beginning of the dinner, claiming that it simply does not taste good. Instead they serve the porridge at the end of the meal as *ris à l'amande,* a cold rice pudding dessert with mounds of whipped cream, chopped almonds, and a cold cherry or raspberry sauce. If *risengrød* is not served at the beginning of dinner, the prized almond, not to be forgotten, is

Christmas Eve services in the Evangelical Lutheran Church begin around five o'clock. The ship model hanging between the chandeliers recalls Denmark's ancient tie to the seas.

hidden in the *ris à l'amande*. The "almond gift," then, will be a pleasant final ceremony to close the Christmas meal.

As the *risengrød* is cleared away, the beautifully browned goose, its platter decorated with miniature Danish flags, is brought in. Goose is the traditional main course for Christmas dinner in Denmark, though there are exceptions. Pork is a likely alternative. In the country, early in the holiday season, a hog is slaughtered, and

every part of it is used to provide holiday dinner fare. Slices of ham, sausage, and head cheese, thus, appear on holiday buffets; these are used in the preparation of *smørrebrød,* the open-faced sandwiches for which the Danes are famous. Venison may also be an alternate choice for the main course on Christmas Eve. The Danes continue to hunt their timberlands for wild deer. But, for the most part, goose, stuffed with apples and prunes, is the most popular entrée on *Juleaften.*

Accompanying the goose on the dinner table are carmel browned potatoes or small potatoes first boiled and then browned in a butter-sugar mixture. Boiled potatoes and gravy from the goose may also be served. Another indispensable item on the Christmas menu is *rødkaal,* or red cabbage. This is prepared in a delicate sweet-sour sauce. With their dinner, Danes may also enjoy *agurkesalat,* a cucumber salad prepared with seedless cucumbers in a vinegar dressing, assorted homemade condiments, such as cucumber pickles, tomato pickles, currant jelly, and ligonberries. Wine generally accompanies a Danish Christmas dinner; this, of course, promotes toasting throughout the meal.

Dessert, if not the delicious *ris à l'amande,* might be *rombudding,* a creamy rum pudding served with chilled raspberry sauce. Another favorite is *aeblekage,* a rich apple crumb cake served under a mound of whipped cream. It has been said the Danes live, eat, and drink better than any other people on earth. Certainly, the *Juleaften* dinner testifies to the validity of this claim.

After Christmas dinner, which typically takes hours, unless hurried along by anxious children, the family remains at the table long enough to sing a song about Mother and all the wonderful things she makes. Father then reads a portion of the Christmas story from the Bible. If one of the children is old enough, he or she may be allowed to give the Bible

Christmas dinner begins upon the family's return home from church on Juleaften. By custom, rice porridge is served before the traditional goose stuffed with apples and prunes is brought to the table.

reading that closes the *Juleaften* dinner.

Finally, the meal is over. While Mother supervises the clearing of the table, Father and perhaps an older brother or sister slip into the parlor to light the tree. In Denmark, a Christmas tree is fir, never pine, and it is illuminated with candles, never with electric lights, which are considered a breach of good taste. Each of the red or white or spiraled candles is carefully lighted, and this takes time. (While the Danes love their Christmas candles, they are not unmindful of the danger.) Meanwhile, the younger children are waiting, in total darkness, outside the parlor doors. Finally, the doors are flung open, and there, in the very center of the room, stands the radiant tree. There is magic in a tree that is lighted with candles. The heat rising from the flames sets the delicate, nearly weightless, paper hearts and flags into a flutter. As they twist on their threads, the golden glow from the mellow candlelight dances over their surface and through the silver tinsel and transparent glass angels and stars. Cones fashioned from metallic gold paper covered with white lace are filled with candies coated with crystallized sugar, which sparkles in the flickering light. The air is filled with the smell of evergreen tempered with the smell of candle wax.

Because the room must be kept cool to ensure that the lighted tree remains fresh, everyone is drawn closer and closer to the warmth of the candles. Finally, the entire family surrounds the tree, and they join hands. As they begin circling the tree, they sing the traditional centuries-old Christmas carols: "High above the tree's green top, the radiance of Christmas beams. . ." and "Lovely is the dark blue sky. . ." or "A child is born in Bethlehem, in Bethlehem. . ." For both young and old, a very favorite Christmas carol is *"Nu har vi Jul igen,"* which means "Now we have Christmas again." The song's second line, "Og Julen varer lige til Paske," can be translated as "And Christmas lasts until Easter." The Danes like to think that this is true.

The dancing, as this circling of the tree in song is called, continues until the family's supply of hymns and carols is exhausted. Throughout this time, a bucket of water or sand has been sitting nearby. The breeze created by the dancing can be dangerous. Everyone keeps a close eye on the candles, which can tip over or fall from their holders.

While the revelers sit and catch their breath and admire the tree, Father may slip out of the room. He returns dressed as *Julemand,* complete with a sackful of gifts flung over his shoulder. Of course, he asks the children if they have been good boys and girls and if they promise to continue this behavior throughout the coming new year. After receiving affirmative answers from all, he opens his sack, distributes the packages, and then goes on his way. After five minutes, Father returns. Even the youngest child of the house, however, is not fooled by this transformation.

Meanwhile the youngsters are eyeing the shining pile of colorful packages under the tree. It is often Father who has the honor of reading the name on each parcel, or he may allow one of the youngest members of the family to present each gift from under the tree. Everyone opens his or her gifts slowly, enjoying each other's delight. In the past, Danish mothers and fathers usually gave a single gift to each child. These were often handmade—a wooden toy, a toy drum, a doll with a china head and china arms, but dressed in clothes made by Mother. Other gifts were more practical—a knitted scarf, hat, or mittens. As the children grew older, they were often allowed to spend their own money on small gifts for the other members of the family. Today, Christmas gifts are little different in Denmark than they are in America: electric trains, electronic games, motorized cars, talking dolls, and Legos®, those wonderful building blocks that are made in Denmark and shipped around the world. But however trends in Christmas gifts have changed through the years, Danish children still enjoy receiving their traditional sweet-filled cone from the Christmas tree. After the candies have been devoured, the beautifully made cones are returned to the tree.

When the excitement ignited by the opening of the gifts has waned somewhat, the family takes a deep breath and sits back for an evening of relaxation. The candles

Finally the parlor doors are opened, revealing, to the entire family, the magic of a **Juletrae** *illuminated with candles.*

on the tree are extinguished, and the tree is moved into a corner. Plates of cookies and cakes are carried into the parlor, and soon the smell of strong, rich coffee joins the smell of evergreen. A bowl of fruits, nuts, candies, *pebbernødder,* and marzipan is passed around the room. No mat-ter how filling the Christmas dinner was, everyone finds room for more sweets.

After coffee, Mother begins to open the Christmas cards and then passes them around the room. The Danes do not open their cards as they arrive in the days before Christmas. They are saved

Singing carols and hymns, the family joins hands and "dances" around the tree.

After exhausting the family repertoire of Christmas music, everyone settles down for the opening of gifts.

for Christmas Eve or Christmas Day. The messages from friends and neighbors, from distant relatives, thus become a special part of the spirit of the day.

On the floor, the children play with their new toys or play games that are a traditional part of Christmas Eve. The older generation explains to the younger how *pebbernødder,* those rock-hard cookies, can be used as tokens or prizes to be won at cards or guessing games. There is no strict bedtime on this night, but as the evening wears on, the smallest children become droopy-eyed and are carried off to bed by Father.

All the Christmas candles around the house are extinguished, and as Mother and Father climb the stairs for bed, they congratulate each other on the beautiful *Juleaften* they have made, on the wonderful memories they have given to their children.

THE
MANY DAYS
OF
CHRISTMAS

December 25 and December 26 are both holidays in Denmark and are called Christmas Day and Second Christmas Day. They are usually spent in an extended celebration with family and friends. "Christmas Day with Grandma and Grandpa Olsen, Second Christmas Day with Grandma and Grandpa Andersen," is often the rule. Both days are occasion for a boisterous, social whirl during which the entire family and many friends join together for fun and feasting.

It is still possible in Denmark to see horse-drawn sleighs bedecked with fancy reins full of jingling bells gliding down snow-covered roads on Christmas Day. Grandparents, on this one day, hitch the horse to the sleigh and drive into town to pick up the "kids." "It's Grandpa Steffensen! He's come to take us back to the farm for Christmas!" The ride out to the country is filled with both excitement and contentment. The children are buried under a cozy eiderdown quilt in the back of the sleigh, their laughter ringing through the crisp, cold air.

Most Danes, of course, have to be satisfied with traveling around on First and Second Christmas in cars, but they do travel, across town and across country. These are days for paying calls and for receiving guests—for sharing the spirit of Christmas. So everyone is up early. Mother prepares a breakfast of warm pumpernickel bread spread with homemade liver paté or the traditional *Julekage*, Christmas coffee cake, with coffee. Another favorite Christmas break-

fast begins with *wienerbrød,* which means "Viennese bread." Curiously, *wienerbrød* is the pastry Americans refer to as "Danish." In Denmark, these sweet rolls are called Viennese because some one hundred years ago, the bakers of Copenhagen went on strike, and bakers from Vienna were hired to replace them. The Viennese bakers used a technique of folding butter into yeast dough that was unknown in Denmark. The people of Copenhagen became so enamored with the Viennese rolls that, after the strike, Danish bakers experimented until they could produce a similar pastry. With time, the bakers of Copenhagen so improved upon the original that the rolls became world-famous as "Danish." To the Danish, however, they are still simply *wienerbrød.*

After breakfast, some families attend a Christmas morning

Christmas is a day for paying calls. If there is sufficient snow, sleighs filled with families on their way to and from visits may still be seen on the streets of rural Danish towns.

church service. But upon return, everyone prepares for the guests who will soon arrive. A sumptuous lunch table is set, a *kolde bord* or a "cold table" that begins about noon, but continues well into the supper hour. This buffet lunch consists of an amazing variety of Danish foods. Nothing is left out. Of course, leftovers are included from the Christmas Eve meal. But there are also meatballs, marinated herring, caviar, shrimp, cold roast pork, salads, liver paté, head cheese, cold meats and sausage, and several varieties of cheese with crackers. A rounded assortment of breads is also available: white, rye, pumpernickel, and *surbrød,* a sort of "gray" bread made with rye flour. With the breads, Danes love to fashion *smørrebrød,* which literally means bread and butter, but, in reality, is an open-faced sandwich piled very high. Atop the butter-spread bread can be added any conceivable combination of foods from the cold table. One needs only a creative imagination to produce a delicious and substantial pyramidal sandwich.

The meal begins with a toast with icy cold *aquavit,* a favorite form of Danish schnapps. *Aquavit* is a traditional Scandinavian liquor distilled from grain or potatoes and flavored with caraway. It is served in thimble-sized glasses and goes with cold foods only. It should never be sipped or left to get warm and is usually followed by a beer chaser. There is a special trick to preparing iced *aquavit.* The bottle is placed in a tall, round, two-quart container of water and set outside to freeze overnight. When dinnertime arrives, the container is removed and the icy *aquavit* is served from within its own block of ice.

Between each course of the meal there is the traditional *skoal* or toast. The Danish toast is a highly formal ritual. It is much more than the simple clink of glasses. With glasses raised, friends look deeply and trustingly into each other's eyes, take a drink, engage looks again, and then put down their glasses. The host always *skoals* first. Guests are then free to toast whenever they wish. But each raising of a glass requires a response. The exchange of trust and warmth between friends and family is the true essence of the ritual. And on *Jul*, nothing could be more appropriate than this warm exchange of friendship. After dinner, the proper response to the host is

"Tak for mad!"—"Thanks for the meal." The host, naturally, replies, *"Velbekommen"*—"You're welcome!" Good manners are held to be important in Denmark and are instilled early in children. Social rituals are taken seriously and are passed from generation to generation.

After hours of Christmas feasting, a long walk in the snow may be in order. Holiday greetings are exchanged with other neighborhood families taking the same exercise. Though a white Christmas in Denmark is always the wish and often the case, it is not an absolute guarantee. The sea, which pokes into bays and coves on every side of the nation, except on the southern border, tends to warm the icy winter winds. No place in Denmark is more than 35 miles from water, and Denmark's climate, particularly on the west coast, is, therefore, milder than

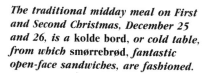

The traditional midday meal on First and Second Christmas, December 25 and 26, is a kolde bord, *or cold table, from which* smørrebrød, *fantastic open-face sandwiches, are fashioned.*

Danes, young and old, play on First Jul and Second Jul. When there is snow, everyone is out-of-doors enjoying the white Christmas, about which Danes are as sentimental as Americans.

might be expected for a country situated so far north. The average winter temperature is 32° F. (0° C.). But Denmark does get its share of snow, and children on Christmas Day enjoy sledding, building snow forts, making snowmen, and throwing snowballs. If there is a frozen pond nearby, there will be ice skaters enjoying the fresh air. If the snow obliges, some families take short, cross-country ski tours in the country, over softly rolling farmland, past captivating windmills, which are as numerous in Denmark as they are in Holland. However, skiing is not as prominent a sport in Denmark as it is in other Scandinavian countries; the country is simply too flat to produce great alpine skiers. If it happens to be a "green" Christmas, a bike ride may be in order. Bicycles are very popular in Denmark. It is not unusual to see a father or mother with one child strapped to a seat on the back of the bike and another seated in a saddle on the crossbar.

In Copenhagen, Denmark's sophisticated capital city situated on the island of Zealand, Christmas Day is a combination of the boisterous and of quiet. While thousands of parties are going on, the streets are also filled with strollers, peacefully admiring their city. Although all businesses—stores, restaurants, theaters, cinemas—are closed on Christmas Day, people are walking, enjoying the crisp air and the city's beautifully picturesque copper-green towers and church spires, which have earned Copenhagen the title, "city of beautiful spires." Christmas shoppers no longer fill *Strøget,* Copenhagen's famous mile-long series of five narrow streets, but on Christmas Day the area is filled with people admiring the decorations, real evergreen festoons that hang between lampposts and across the streets. Window shoppers gaze at the brilliant displays that fill the windows of some of the world's finest shops. The showrooms of Royal Copenhagen porcelain and its rival Bing and Grøndahl, as well as the world-renowned silver shop of Georg Jensen, are found in the *Strøget* district. On Christmas Day, the *Langelinie,* the half-mile promenade along Copenhagen's harbor, is filled with walkers, taking the air and working off their Christmas lunches. At the end of this walk is the famous life-sized statue, cast in bronze, of Hans Christian Andersen's *Little Mermaid.* She sits on a smooth boulder just beyond the shore, perennially watching the ships that come and go, presenting to the world a symbol of Denmark's special, fairyland quality.

Another famous sight in Copenhagen, and one which occurs every day of the year at noon, is the colorful changing of the guard at Amalienborg Palace, the residence of Denmark's Queen Margrethe II. Although the Queen and her family spend the holidays at Marselisborg Palace in Århus, the changing of the guard takes place as usual. The 36 impressive guardsmen marching through the snow-covered streets in their towering bearskin shakos, with their swords flashing at their sides, look like toy soldiers—a perfect touch for Christmas in a fairyland.

After watching the changing of the guard, families return home for deliciously warm *jule gløgg,* a spicy Christmas punch, or for coffee and cookies and sweets. The tree is relighted in anticipation that guests may drop in or, perhaps, the last of the Christmas cards will be opened and passed around the room so that everyone may share in the spirit of *Jul* on this night.

Second Christmas Day, December 26, in Denmark is very much like First Christmas Day. The other side of the family is visited, or friends or family seen on Christmas simply reciprocate the previous day's hospitality. Thus, there is another round of feasting and fun. Although the stores are

not yet open, restaurants and theaters open their doors on Second Christmas. Many theaters in Copenhagen and smaller cities stage a premiere, and the house is filled with people dressed in evening clothes. Other theaters present the same play each year during the Christmas season. The *Folketeatret* in Copenhagen has produced *Christmas in Nøeddebo Rectory* every Christmas season since 1888. A new theater manager at the *Folketeatret* knows it would be folly to change the bill. No one tampers with Danish Christmas traditions, and *Christmas in Nøeddebo Rectory* has become as traditionally a part of Christmas in Copenhagen as *A Christmas Carol* is a part of the holiday season in Great Britain and America.

By December 27, business throughout Denmark returns to

A country defined by water, Denmark, like Holland, is dotted with windmills, which drain precious land for cultivation and grazing. The resulting canals and ponds combined with Denmark's long winters have produced a nation on skates.

normal. Stores open their doors for the onslaught of gift-exchanging, and most Danes return to their work. However, should the three-day Christmas celebration fall just before a weekend, the celebration and visiting can continue for five straight days.

Through the week between Christmas and New Year's, Danish children are still enjoying their school holiday recess, and many adults take vacations at this time of the year. The children never tire of playing outdoors, especially if there is snow. And, of course, there are parties and visits still going on. Everyone must see who has the prettiest Christmas tree.

Workers' unions, farming organizations, and other groups throughout Denmark sponsor holiday parties that are modeled after traditional *Juletraefests. Juletraefests,* or Christmas-tree parties, were originally town parties, held in the village or town hall, on an evening during Christmas week. All townspeople were invited, and it was an evening to which everyone looked forward. Mothers sewed new party dresses, complete with matching hair ribbons, for their daughters, and new clothes were made for the boys as well. On the way to the party, children stopped at the homes of old people, who were not attending the *Juletraefest,* to show off their finery. The town hall was decorated for the occasion, and in the center of the floor was a huge candlelit Christmas tree. Everyone, young and old, parents, grandparents, and children, joined hands and sang and danced around the tree. Later

Hans Christian Andersen's Little Mermaid, cast in bronze, is found at the end of the Langelinie, *a favorite promenade along Copenhagen's quay-lined harbor.*

in the evening, an orchestra played waltzes, polkas, folk and square dances. Grown-ups danced with children. No one sat out. There was punch and Christmas sweets throughout the night, and at the end, each child received an orange, an apple, and a box of Christmas candy to take home.

As more people moved off the farm and from small villages into large cities, the *Juletraefests* were, for the most part, no longer given. But a Christmas tradition is a tradition, and the Danes missed the town parties. Eventually organizations began to sponsor *Juletraefests*. So the custom did not die. It was transformed into a kind of office party that included the entire family. These are usually held during Christmas week and are staged in hotels or restaurants. Danish children, thus, anticipate these parties exactly as their parents and grandparents did.

Although festive gatherings and visits for many Danes continue throughout Christmas week, the next formally celebrated holiday is *Nytaarsaften,* New Year's Eve. This is an evening of true merrymaking throughout the country. In many Danish homes, *Nytaarsaften* is spent in a traditional manner with a small gathering of family and friends. Dinner on this night may include boiled codfish with a mus-

Originally, Juletraefests, *Christmas tree parties, were village dances, where young and old shared in the good cheer of* Jul. *As Denmark has become more urbanized,* Juletraefests *have become union and office parties for the families of co-workers. The spirit of the* fests, *however, remains the same.*

Danes love good food and hospitality. On New Year's Eve the nation turns out to welcome in the new year. Restaurants and hotel dining rooms provide dancing and lavish buffets.

tard sauce, smoked pork loin, white cabbage in a cream sauce, or more of the famous *smørre-brød*. After dinner, the family may play cards or table games with the children. The candles on the Christmas tree are relighted, possibly for the last time before the tree is dismantled, and carols may be sung. At midnight, as church bells toll and town clocks chime all across the nation, there is spirited noisemaking, even fireworks in the yard, and then a toast to the new year.

In years past, farmers throughout the countryside shot off their guns as part of the noise-making. According to an ancient superstition, the more noise with which the new year is ushered in, the more likely it is that evil spirits will be frightened away. Farmhands made *gubbepotte*, or a rumble pot, with which to add to

the evening's din. A *gubbepotte* was made from a large can. Over the opening, a pig's bladder was stretched. A piece of hollow pipe was then placed in the middle, and when the pipe was rubbed up and down, a loud rumbling or moaning noise was created.

Today, many Danes prefer to dine out on New Year's Eve, and it is usually very difficult to find an empty table without a reservation. Elegant restaurants and hotel dining rooms are filled to capacity.

But for many Danes, New Year's Eve is often far less formal than dinner in a hotel dining room. The younger set attends parties with food and fun, streamers, champagne, and fireworks. The neighborhood streets are filled with young people on their way to the festivities. And on *Nytaarsaften*, pranks and tricks are the rule. People hammer at doors and knock at windows wishing everyone within a *"Godt Nytaar"*—Happy New Year! Revelers are often invited in for a New Year's toast or some pastry and coffee. But this does not protect one from tricks. Woe to anyone who forgets to protect his belongings! Everything outdoors that is not nailed down must either be brought in or lost. Garden gates are strung up on flagpoles, wheelbarrows are perched on garage roofs, farm wagons are dismantled, and bicycles are hoisted onto trees. In the past when fireworks displays were held at midnight in the *raadhuspladsen,* or town hall square, people often spied their belongings in the center of a bonfire ready to be torched. It was New Year's Eve, and one simply had to be philosophical about these things.

Such pranks are not, by any means, limited to the past, nor are they limited to the young. Practical jokes occur at most New Year's Eve gatherings, whether the guests are young or old. A party of middle-aged couples might include the following scenario: The hostess has finished serving her guests the usual *jule gløgg,* marinated herring, cheese, and a variety of other hors d'oeuvres. It is time for coffee, but the coffee pot is missing. Although it is New Year's Eve, the hostess is not amused. Entertaining is a serious business, and coffee must be served. As she frantically searches the kitchen, her guests begin to giggle. They know perfectly well that someone has taken her coffee pot and hidden it. The question is, "Who took

"Godt Nytaar, skoal!" *"May you prosper throughout the new year!"*

it, and where is it?" The search now takes on the aspect of a scavenger hunt. Everyone present goes home and hunts through their own cupboards for the missing pot. It turns up, of course, as everyone knew it would, in someone else's kitchen. At the beginning of the party, one of the guests filched the pot, sneaked out, and hid it, not in his or her kitchen, but in one of the other guest's cupboards. The coffee pot is returned to the hostess, the coffee is brewed, and the party continues. All the while, everyone is trying to guess the identity of the practical joker. In Denmark, New Year's Eve is not dull.

The mischief-makers in the streets, their escapades completed,

also return to their parties. The dancing and the celebration continues well into the wee hours of the morning.

An annual event on New Year's Eve is the Queen's New Year's address to the country, which is broadcast nationally on television. The Queen, Margrethe II, and her family return to Copenhagen from their Christmas holiday in Århus in order to host, at Amalienborg Palace, a lavish New Year's Eve banquet for numerous national and foreign dignitaries. The five-to ten-minute speech, televised directly from the banquet, usually occurs as early as 6:00 in the evening, and most Danes make a special effort to listen to her remarks. Besides offering a New

In a gilded, royal coach, Queen Margrethe II and her consort Prince Henrik are transported to Amalienborg Palace for the New Year's Eve state banquet. From this annual reception, the Queen addresses the people of Denmark on the state of the Kingdom.

After the frenetic pace of Christmas in Denmark, a walk through the silent, snow-laced woods caps the **Jul** *season with peace and renewal.*

Year's message to her subjects, the Queen usually discusses the state of the nation's affairs. Later in the evening, around 7:30 P.M., the prime minister, who holds the real political power in Denmark, also delivers a televised speech to the country.

The Christmas season in Denmark ends officially on January 5, Twelfth-night, the eve of Epiphany, commonly called the Three Holy Kings' Day. The few Christmas trees still left standing in some Danish houses are taken down on this day. Of course, most trees have already been dismantled and placed in the garden, where the birds can feed on the suet and nuts that have been hung from the boughs. As a substitute for the now retired Christmas tree, many Danes light three candles on Twelfth-night, one for each of the Three Wise Men.

And so Christmas in Denmark is over—at least for another year. The last remnants of the joyous Yuletide season are removed. Children return to their schools, and lessons begin again in earnest. Mothers and fathers return to their jobs. It has been a wonderful few weeks—a Christmas season to remember. And it is, of course, these memories of personal joy and family unity—these remembrances of Christmas past—that fuel the anticipation of, as well as the preparation for, next year's *Jul,* that time of fantasy in the fairy-land Kingdom of Denmark.

THE FAIRYLAND

enmark has been called a fairyland. And as one travels through the well-tended fields of the countryside, one begins to believe that this country is indeed a fantasy. Ancient, moated castles loom over dark, beech forests, and immaculate white farm buildings flank meadows startlingly green and peaceful. Villages filled with old, crooked, half-timbered cottages are inhabited by people who smile and say, "*Got dag*," ("Good day") to strangers they meet along the narrow, cobbled streets. Storks, which arrive from Egypt in the spring, nest atop chimneys that cast twisting shadows across thatched roofs. Wild swans silently glide among water lilies floating on the surface of deep ponds.

The cities, which rise up out of green fields and the bluer green sea, are crowned with fantastic spires fashioned like giant dragons sculpted in mottled copper. There is a queen who resides in a baroque palace protected by guardsmen in tall, bearskin hats. There is a place called Tivoli, a dreamland of pagodas, Chinese temples, and mosques out of the Arabian Nights, that is set in the center of a city of fountains and amid neat rows of houses painted pink and beige and powder blue. Black-faced chimney sweeps in battered top hats and red-coated mailmen on yellow bicycles patiently wait while a policeman stops traffic to allow a duck and her ducklings to portage from one canal to another. It's as if all of Denmark were the invention of Hans Christian Andersen. Or was it

the other way around? Were Hans Christian Andersen's tales the invention of Denmark?

The Danes call him H. C. Andersen, and he is a national hero. He viewed his own life as a fairy tale and his beloved Denmark as a fairyland, and he pictured it as such to the world. It is nearly impossible to separate Andersen's vision of Denmark from the reality, for the reality is, in fact, fantastic. Wherever one travels in Denmark, one sees his characters and his settings: the castles; and the ducks that stop traffic; the pagodas; the guardsmen who look like toy soldiers; the cottages inhabited by polite, kindly people, the wild swans; the Queen in her palace; the chimney sweep toting his ladder over one shoulder; and, of course, the storks that guard their nests exactly as Andersen described them.

A statue of Hans Christian Andersen in Odense, the storyteller's birthplace.

H. C. Andersen's fairyland is not, however, all goodness and light. There is a dark side, a nether world populated with mischievous dwarfs and forbidding snow queens, with wicked trolls and vicious dogs that dwell deep below the earth. It is this contrast between the light and the dark that creates the tension that fills Andersen's stories with mystery and pathos. And this contrast is something that the Danes understand better, perhaps, about Andersen's work than his other readers. The contrast between the light and the dark is part of their heritage, their folklore. It is the same contrast that is the essence of the Danish *Jul:* the long, gloomy nights of December brightened by the light of so many candles; the *nisser,* the spirits of *Jul,* who are, in some way, related to the devil, and who, on Christmas Eve, must be appeased with a bowl of porridge; *Jul,* the ancient festival of Odin and of the dead, that was transformed by Christianity into Christmas, a festival of birth. The same contrasts—the light and the dark, goodness and evil, birth and death—that are the focus of a Danish Christmas are the focus of Andersen's fairy tales.

H. C. Andersen was born 150 years ago in the city of Odense, a name that means "shrine of Odin." The son of a shoemaker, who wanted to be a scholar, and a washerwoman, who believed in ghosts and spirits from the underworld, Andersen was greatly influenced by both parents. He grew up to be both erudite and superstitious, sophisticated and

provincial, a man of contrasts. His childhood was spent in abject poverty as well as loneliness, a past most people would choose to forget. Andersen, however, remembered it all and used it all in his stories, many of which can be interpreted as autobiographical.

The father, like the son, was something of a dreamer. He built for young Hans a puppet theater, taught the boy how to cut silhouettes from paper, and read to his son from the *Arabian Nights.* The boy learned early to retreat into this world of make-believe. Filled with contrasts, the boy became both morbidly sensitive and a show-off. He walked through the streets of Odense singing, basking in the attention he received for his beautiful, soprano voice.

When the father died, Andersen's mother told her 11-year-old son that his father had been taken by the "snow queen," a mythical figure that Andersen characterized in one of his most famous stories as beautiful, but cold and uncaring. Andersen's relationship with his father may also have been the basis of *The Red Shoes,* the story of a penniless, young girl who, after seeing a princess in a pair of red shoes, becomes obsessed with owning a pair of her own. Eventually, she is outfitted, by a cobbler, with the identical shoes, which she wears to church, scandalizing the congregation. Because of her vanity, the slippers are bewitched by one of those dark characters that haunt Andersen's tales. Unable to remove the shoes, the little girl must dance—forever! In the end, she begs a woodcutter to chop off her feet at the ankles. Cleansed of earthly vanity, she ascends to heaven and finds the peace she could not find on earth. *The Red Shoes* is a disturbing story that may be read as both a lesson on life as well as an allegory of Andersen's own experiences. As a very young boy, H. C. Andersen stepped into the red shoes of ambition and was never able to step out of them again. He achieved both great fame and wealth, but the peace and happiness of a family and home, which he desperately desired, eluded him throughout life.

At 14, Andersen left home for Copenhagen to seek fame and fortune on the stage. He intended to be a dancer and a singer, as well as an actor. His ambitions were boundless. Unfortunately, he was clumsy. His beautiful soprano voice was beginning to change, and he was already too tall and gangly to play juvenile roles. He was also homely with a shockingly large nose. The country boy was simply laughed at in the city. His dreams were ridiculed by the sophisticated troupe of actors at the Royal Theater.

Then as now, gauche, homely people rarely achieve distinction on the stage. The public prefers swans to ugly ducklings. Andersen nearly starved before he met peo-

Ladder-toting chimney sweeps continue to ply their trade in the double-breasted tunic and top hat that Andersen described in The Shepherdess and the Chimneysweep, *a story of porcelain figurines who peek over the top of a chimney, decide they are too delicate for the world, and return to their tabletop.*

ple who helped him. A scholarship was arranged to a state grammar school, but this also proved to be a painful experience for the provincial boy. Humiliated by the masters for his ignorance and country manners, Andersen despised school. He did, however, remain long enough to acquire an education as well as an ambition to write. Eventually, he returned to Copenhagen and published a poem, "The Dying Child," which won him international literary recognition. An amazing volume and variety of work followed: poetry, plays, novels, travel books.

In 1835, he published *Fairy Tales Told for Children*, four stories that he dashed off to earn extra money. He never imagined that the fairy tales, which he con-

sidered a trifle, would eclipse his serious work. A second volume of tales soon followed the first. Eventually, H. C. Andersen published a new book of fairy tales nearly every year for the rest of his life. He had, at last, achieved distinction. The whole world knew his name. Celebrities courted him. Charles Dickens pronounced Andersen a genius. Heads of state consulted him. He dined with kings and queens. The ugly duckling was transformed into a swan.

Andersen, however, remained the lonely outsider. He fell in love at least a half a dozen times, but women found him unappealing. On one of his many tours through Europe, Andersen met and fell in love with Jenny Lind, the Swedish nightingale. Although she spurned

Modeled after the guards before Amalienborg Palace, Andersen's brave toy soldier's single devotion was to duty. The Palace Guard, to the man, defended their King before the oncoming tanks during the German invasion of Denmark.

his advances, they became close friends. It is believed that Andersen's story, *The Nightingale,* is a reflection of his affection for the singer.

H. C. Andersen died in 1875 and was buried in Copenhagen. The small stone over his grave is inscribed simply, *Digteren,* The Poet. It is a fitting monument. Andersen described himself as "the most Danish of Danish writers." And it is *his* vision of Denmark, his fairyland, that the world sees when visiting Andersen's beloved homeland.

Two of H. C. Andersen's tales follow. Both are *Jul* stories, and like Christmas in Denmark, they are studies in contrast, filled with both darkness and light. The little fir tree is transformed into a glittering Christmas tree, but is far too busy worrying about tomorrow to appreciate today. The story of-

fers a lesson Andersen may have learned through his own experiences.

Cold and hungry on New Year's Eve, the little match girl, attempting to keep warm, ignites her matches and sees visions of beauty and love in the flames. Perhaps the Danes see similar visions in the flames of their many *Jul* candles. It is certain they find such visions in the words of their beloved poet, H. C. Andersen.

Pantomime and masque, dramatic forms that date back to before the Renaissance, continue to find an audience in the Copenhagen theater. Andersen, at 14, left home for Copenhagen to become an actor. Failing, he turned to writing tales filled with the same mix of fantasy and message he had learned so early from the traditions of Danish theater.

THE FIR TREE

by Hans Christian Andersen

FAR DOWN IN THE FOREST, WHERE THE WARM SUN AND THE FRESH AIR made a sweet resting place, grew a pretty little fir tree. And yet it was not so happy—it wished so much to be tall like its companions, the pines and firs which grew around it. The sun shone, the soft air fluttered its leaves, and the little peasant children passed by, prattling merrily, but the fir tree heeded them not. Sometimes children would bring a large basket of raspberries or strawberries, wreathed on a straw, and seat themselves near the fir tree and say, "Is it not a pretty little tree?" which made it feel more unhappy than before.

And yet all this while the tree grew a notch or joint taller every year—for by the number of joints in the stem of a fir tree we can discover its age. Still, as it grew it complained, "Oh, how I wish I were as tall as the other trees. Then I would spread out my branches on every side, and my top would overlook the wide world. I should have the birds building their nests on my boughs, and when the wind blew, I should bow with stately dignity like my tall companions."

The tree was so discontented that it took no pleasure in the warm sunshine, the birds, or the rosy clouds that floated over it morning and evening. Sometimes in winter, when the snow lay white and glittering on the ground, a hare would come springing along and would jump right over the little tree, and then how mortified it would feel!

Two winters passed; and when the third arrived, the tree had grown so tall that the hare was obliged to run round it. Yet it remained dissatisfied and would exclaim, "Oh, if I could but keep on growing tall and old! There is nothing else worth caring for in the world."

In the autumn, as usual, the woodcutters came and cut down several of the tallest trees. And the young fir tree, which was not grown to its full height, shuddered as the noble trees fell to the earth with a crash. After the branches were lopped off, the trunks looked so slender and bare that they could scarcely be recognized. Then they were placed upon wagons and drawn by horses out of the forest. "Where were they going? What would become of them?" The young fir tree wished very much to know. So in the spring, when the swallows and the storks came, it asked, "Do you know where those trees were taken? Did you meet them?"

The swallows knew nothing, but the stork, after a little reflection, nodded his head and said, "Yes, I think I do. I met several new ships when I flew from Egypt, and they had fine masts that smelt like fir. I think these must have been the trees. I assure you they were stately, very stately."

"Oh, how I wish I were tall enough to go on the sea," said the fir tree. "What is this sea, and what does it look like?"

"It would take too much time to explain," said the stork, flying quickly away.

"Rejoice in thy youth," said the sunbeam. "Rejoice in thy fresh growth and the young life that is in thee." And the wind kissed the tree and the dew watered it with tears, but the fir tree regarded them not.

Christmas drew near and many young trees were cut down, some even smaller and younger than the fir tree, who enjoyed neither rest nor peace from longing to leave its forest home. These young trees, chosen for their beauty, kept their branches, but they too were laid on wagons and drawn by horses out of the forest.

"Where are they going?" asked the fir tree. "They are no taller than I am. Indeed, one is much shorter. And why are the branches not cut off? Where are they going?"

"We know. We know," sang the sparrows. "We have looked in at the windows of the houses in town, and we know what is done with them. They are dressed up in the most splendid manner. We have seen them standing in the middle of a warm room, and adorned with all sorts of beautiful things—honey cakes, gilded apples, playthings, and many hundreds of wax tapers."

"And then," asked the fir tree, trembling through all its branches, "and then what happens?"

"We did not see any more," said the sparrows. "But that was enough for us."

"I wonder whether anything so brilliant will ever happen to me," thought the fir tree. "It would be much better than crossing the sea. I long for it almost with pain. Oh, when will Christmas be here? I am now as tall and well grown as those which were taken away last year. Oh, that I were now laid on the wagon, or standing in the warm room, with all that brightness and splendor around me! Something better and more beautiful is to come after, or the trees would not be so decked out. Yes, what follows will be grander and more splendid. What can it be? I am weary with longing. I scarcely know how I feel."

"Rejoice with us," said the air and the sunlight. "Enjoy thine own bright life in the fresh air."

But the tree would not rejoice, though it grew taller every day. And winter and summer its dark green foliage might be seen in the forest, while passers-by would say, "What a beautiful tree!"

A short time before Christmas, the discontented fir tree was the first to fall. As the ax cut through the stem and divided the pith, the tree fell with a groan to the earth, conscious of pain and faintness, and forgetting all its anticipations of happiness in sorrow at leaving its home in the forest. It knew that it should never again see its dear old companions, the trees, nor the little bushes and many-colored flowers that had grown by its side; perhaps not even the birds. Neither was the journey at all pleasant. The tree first recovered itself

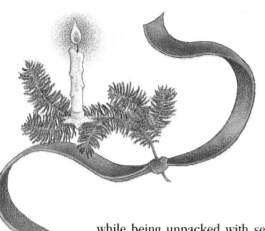

while being unpacked with several other trees in the courtyard of a house, and it heard a man say, "We want only one, and this is the prettiest."

Then came two servants in grand livery and carried the fir tree into a large and beautiful apartment. On the walls hung pictures and near the great stove stood great china vases, with lions on the lids. There were rocking chairs, silken sofas, and large tables covered with pictures, books, and playthings worth a great deal of money. At least, the children said so. Then the fir tree was placed in a large tub full of sand, but green baize hung all around it so that no one could see it was a tub, and it stood on a very handsome carpet. How the fir tree trembled! "What is going to happen to me now?" Some young ladies came and the servants helped them to adorn the tree. On one branch they hung little bags cut out of colored paper, and each bag was filled with sweetmeats. From other branches hung gilded apples and walnuts as if they had grown there. And above and all around were hundreds of red, blue, and white tapers, which were fastened on the branches. Dolls exactly like real babies were placed under the green leaves—the tree had never seen such things before! And at the very top was fastened a glittering star made of tinsel. Oh, it was very beautiful!

"This evening," they all exclaimed, "how bright it will be!" "Oh, that the evening were here!" thought the tree. "And the tapers lighted! Then I shall know what else is going to happen. Will the trees of the forest come to see me? I wonder if the sparrows will peep in at the windows as they fly? Shall I grow faster here, and keep on all these ornaments during summer and winter?" But guessing was of very little use. It made the fir tree's bark ache, and this pain is as bad for a tree as a headache is for us. At last the tapers were lighted and then what a glistening blaze of light the tree presented! It trembled so with joy in all its branches that one of the candles fell among the green leaves and burnt some of them. "Help! Help!" exclaimed the young ladies, but there was no danger, for they quickly extinguished the fire. After this the tree tried not to tremble at all, though the fire frightened it. It was so anxious not to hurt any of the beautiful ornaments, even while their brilliancy dazzled it. And now the folding doors were thrown open and a troop of children rushed in as if they intended to upset the tree. They were followed more slowly by their elders. For a moment the little ones stood silent with astonishment, and then they shouted for joy till the room rang, and they danced merrily round the tree, while one present after another was taken from it.

"What are they doing? What will happen next?" thought the fir. At last the candles burnt down to the branches and were put out. Then the children received permission to plunder the tree.

Oh, how they rushed upon it, till the branches cracked, and had it not been fastened with the glistening star to the ceiling, it would have been thrown down. The children then danced about with their pretty toys, and no one noticed the tree

except the children's maid, who came and peeped among the branches to see if an apple or a fig had been forgotten.

"A story! A story!" cried the children, pulling a little fat man towards the tree.

"Now we shall be in the green shade," said the man, as he seated himself under it, "and the tree will have the pleasure of hearing also. But I shall only relate one story. What shall it be? Ivede-Avede? Or Humpty Dumpty, who fell downstairs but soon got up again, and at last married a princess?"

"Ivede-Avede," cried some. "Humpty Dumpty," cried others, and there was a fine shouting and crying out. The fir tree remained quite still and thought to itself, "Shall I have anything to do with all this?" But it had already amused them as much as they wished. Then the old man told them the story of Humpty Dumpty—how he fell downstairs, and was raised up again, and married a princess. And the children clapped their hands and cried, "Tell another! Tell another!" They wanted to hear the story of Ivede-Avede, but they only had Humpty Dumpty. After this the fir tree became quite silent and thoughtful. Never had the birds in the forest told such tales as Humpty Dumpty, who fell downstairs and yet married a princess.

"Ah, yes, so it happens in the world," thought the fir tree who believed it all, because it was related by such a nice man. "Ah, well," it thought, "who knows? Perhaps I may fall down too, and marry a princess." And it looked forward joyfully to the next evening, expecting to be again decked out with lights and playthings, gold and fruit. "Tomorrow I will not tremble," it thought. "I will enjoy all my splendor, and I shall hear the story of Humpty Dumpty again, and perhaps Ivede-Avede." And the tree remained quiet and thoughtful all night. In the morning the servants and the housemaid came in.

"Now," thought the fir, "all my splendor is going to begin again." But they dragged it out of the room and upstairs to the garret and threw it on the floor, in a dark corner where no daylight shone, and there they left it. "What does this mean?" thought the tree. "What am I to do here? I can hear nothing in a place like this!" And it leaned against the wall and thought and thought.

It had time enough to think, for days and nights passed and no one came near it, and when at last somebody did come, it was only to put away large boxes in a corner. So the tree was completely hidden from sight as if it had never existed. "It is winter now," thought the tree. "The ground is hard and covered with snow, so that people cannot plant me. I shall be sheltered here, I daresay, until spring comes. How thoughtful and kind everybody is to me! Still I wish this place were not so dark as well as lonely, with not even a little hare to look at. How pleasant it was out in the forest when the snow lay on the ground. Then the hare would run by, yes, and jump over me too, although I did not like it then. Oh, it is terribly lonely here!"

"Squeak, squeak," said a little mouse, creeping cautiously towards the tree. Then came another, and they both

sniffed at the fir tree and crept between the branches.

"Oh, it is very cold," said the little mouse, "or else we should be so comfortable here, shouldn't we, you old fir tree?"

"I am not old," said the fir tree. "There are many who are older than I am."

"Where do you come from and what do you know?" asked the mice, who were full of curiosity. "Have you seen the most beautiful places in the world, and can you tell us all about them? And have you been in the storeroom, where cheeses lie on the shelf and hams hang from the ceiling? One can run about on tallow candles there, and go in thin and come out fat."

"I know nothing of that place," said the fir tree. "But I know the wood where the sun shines and the birds sing." And then the tree told the little mice all about its youth. They had never heard such an account in their lives. After they had listened to it attentively, they said, "What a number of things you have seen! You must have been very happy."

"Happy?" exclaimed the fir tree. And then as it reflected upon what it had been telling them, it said, "Ah, yes. After all, those were happy days." But when it went on and related all about Christmas Eve, and how it had been dressed up with cakes and lights, the mice said, "How happy you must have been, you old fir tree!"

"I am not old at all," replied the tree. "I only came from the forest this winter. I am now checked in my growth."

"What splendid stories you can relate," said the little mice. And the next

night four other mice came with them to hear what the tree had to tell. The more it talked, the more it remembered, and then it thought to itself, "Those were happy days, but they may come again. Humpty Dumpty fell downstairs, and yet he married the princess. Perhaps I may marry a princess too." And the fir tree thought of the pretty little birch tree that grew in the forest, which was to it a real, beautiful princess.

"Who is Humpty Dumpty?" asked the little mice, and then the tree related the whole story. It could remember every single word, and the little mice were so delighted with it that they were ready to jump to the top of the tree. The next night a great many more mice came, and on Sunday two rats came with them. But the rats said it was not a pretty story at all, and the little mice were very sorry, for it made them also think less of it.

"Do you know only one story?" asked the rats.

"Only one," replied the fir tree. "I heard it on the happiest evening in my life, but I did not know I was so happy at the time."

"We think it is a very miserable story," said the rats. "Don't you know any story about bacon or tallow in the storeroom?"

"No," replied the tree.

"Many thanks to you then," replied the rats, and they marched off.

The little mice also kept away after this, and the tree sighed and said, "It was very pleasant when the merry little mice

sat round me and listened while I talked. Now that is all past too. However, I shall consider myself happy when someone comes to take me out of this place." But would this ever happen? Yes, one morning people came to clear out the garret. The boxes were packed away, and the tree was pulled out of the corner and thrown roughly on the garret floor. Then the servant dragged it out upon the staircase where the daylight shone.

"Now life is beginning again," said the tree, rejoicing in the sunshine and fresh air. Then it was carried downstairs and taken into the courtyard so quickly that it forgot to think of itself, and could only look about. There was so much to be seen! The court was close to a garden, where everything was blooming. Fresh and fragrant roses hung over the little palings. The linden trees were in blossom, while the swallows flew here and there, crying, "Twit, twit, twit, my mate is coming." But it was not the fir tree they meant.

"Now I shall live," cried the tree, joyfully spreading out its branches. But alas, they were all withered and yellow, and it lay in a corner among weeds and nettles. The star of gold paper still stuck in the top of the tree and glittered in the sunshine.

In the same courtyard were playing two of the merry children who had danced round the tree at Christmas and had been so happy. The youngest saw the gilded star and ran and pulled it off the tree.

"Look what is sticking to the old ugly fir tree," said the child, treading on the branches till they crackled under his boots. And the tree saw all the fresh bright flowers in the garden, and then looked at itself and wished it had remained in the dark corner of the garret. It thought of its fresh youth in the forest, of the merry Christmas evening, and of the little mice who had listened to the story of Humpty Dumpty.

"Past! past!" said the old tree. "Oh, had I but enjoyed myself while I could have done so! Now it is too late!"

Then a lad came and chopped the tree into small pieces, till a large bundle lay in a heap on the ground. The pieces were placed in a fire under the kettle, and they quickly blazed up brightly, while the tree sighed so deeply that each sigh was like a little pistol shot. Then the children, who were at play, came and seated themselves in front of the fire, and looked at it and cried, "Pop! pop!" But at each "Pop!" which was a deep sigh, the tree was thinking of a summer day in the forest, or of some winter night there when the stars shone brightly, and of Christmas evening, and of Humpty Dumpty, the only story it had ever heard or knew how to relate— till at last it was consumed.

The boys still played in the garden, and the youngest wore on his breast the golden star with which the tree had been adorned during the happiest evening of its existence. Now all was past: the tree's life was past, and the story also—for all stories must come to an end at last.

THE LITTLE MATCH GIRL

by Hans Christian Andersen

IT WAS LATE ON A BITTERLY COLD NEW YEAR'S EVE. THE SNOW WAS FALLING. A poor little girl was wandering in the dark cold streets; she was bareheaded and barefoot. She had of course had slippers on when she left home, but they were not much good, for they were so huge. They had last been worn by her mother, and they fell off the poor little girl's feet when she was running across the street to avoid two carriages that were rolling rapidly by. One of the shoes could not be found at all, and the other was picked up by a boy who ran off with it, saying that it would do for a cradle when he had some children of his own.

So the poor little girl had to walk on with her little bare feet, which were red and blue with the cold. She carried a quantity of matches in her old apron, and held a packet of them in her hand.

Nobody had bought any of her matches during all the long day, and nobody had even given her a copper. The poor little creature was hungry and perishing with cold, and she looked the picture of misery.

The snowflakes fell on her long yellow hair, which curled so prettily round her face, but she paid no attention to that. Lights were shining from every window, and there was a most delicious odor of roast goose in the streets, for it was New Year's Eve. She could not forget that! She found a corner where one house projected a little beyond the next one, and here she crouched, drawing up her feet under her, but she was colder than ever. She did not dare to go home, for she had not sold any matches and had not earned a single penny. Her father would beat her, and besides it was almost as cold at home as it was here. They had only the roof over them, and the wind whistled through it although they stuffed up the biggest cracks with rags and straw.

Her little hands were almost dead with cold. Oh, one little match would do some good! If she only dared, she would pull one out of the packet and strike it on the wall to warm her fingers. She pulled out one. *R-r-sh-sh!* How it sputtered and blazed! It burnt with a bright clear flame, just like a little candle, when she held her hand round it.

Now the light seemed very strange to her! The little girl fancied that she was sitting in front of a big stove with polished brass feet and handles. There was a splendid fire blazing in it and warming her so beautifully, but—what happened? Just as she was stretching out her feet to warm them, the flame went out, the stove vanished—and she was left sitting with the end of the burnt match in her hand.

She struck a new one. It burnt, it blazed up, and where the light fell upon the wall, it became transparent like gauze, and she could see right through it into the room.

The table was spread with a snowy cloth and pretty china. A roast goose stuffed with apples and prunes was steaming on it. And what was even better, the goose hopped from the dish with the carving knife sticking in his back and waddled across the floor. It came right up to the poor child, and then—the match went out, and there was nothing to be seen but the thick black wall.

She lit another match. This time she was sitting under a lovely Christmas tree. It was much bigger and more beautifully decorated than the one she had seen when she peeped through the glass doors at the rich merchant's house on the last Christmas. Thousands of lighted candles gleamed under its branches. And colored pictures, such as she had seen in the shop windows, looked down at her. The little girl stretched out both her hands towards them—then out went the match. All the Christmas candles rose higher and higher, till she saw that they were only the twinkling stars. One of them fell and made a bright streak of light across the sky.

"Now someone is dying," thought the little girl, for her old grandmother, the only person who had ever been kind to her, used to say, "When a star falls, a soul is going up to God."

Now she struck another match against the wall, and this time it was her grandmother who appeared in the circle of flame. She saw her quite clearly and distinctly, looking so gentle and happy.

"Grandmother!" cried the little creature. "Oh, do take me with you. I know you will vanish when the match goes out. You will vanish like the warm stove, the delicious goose, and the beautiful Christmas tree!"

She hastily struck a whole bundle of matches, because she did so long to keep her grandmother with her. The light of the matches made it as bright as day. Grandmother had never before looked so big or so beautiful. She lifted the little girl up in her arms, and they soared in a halo of light and joy, far, far above the earth, where there was no more cold, no hunger, and no pain—for they were with God.

In the cold morning light the poor little girl sat there, in the corner between the houses, with rosy cheeks and a smile on her face—dead. Frozen to death on the last night of the old year. New Year's Day broke on the little body still sitting with the ends of the burnt-out matches in her hand.

"She must have tried to warm herself," they said. Nobody knew what beautiful visions she had seen, nor in what a halo she had entered with her grandmother upon the glories of the New Year.

♣♥♣♥ DANISH CRAFTS ♥♣♥♣

Basket-weave Heart

Materials

- sheet of red and sheet of white construction paper
  (Scraps of red and white felt may also be used.)
- scissors*
- stapler

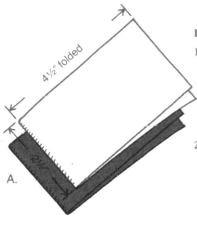

A.

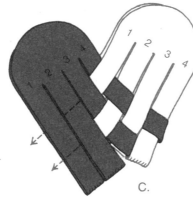

C.

Instructions

1. Cut a rectangle 2½ inches by 9 inches from the red and from the white construction paper (or felt).

2. Fold the rectangles in half. The folded sheets should be 2½ inches by 4½ inches.

3. From both the red and white rectangles, cut, up from the fold, three 3-inch slits (*see* Diagram B).

4. Opposite the fold, round off the top (*see* Diagram B).

B.

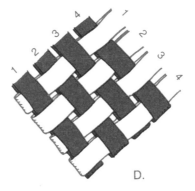

D.

5. Insert the first loop of the white through the fourth loop of the red (*see* Diagram C). Note: The loops are woven *through*, not under, each other. Loop #1 of the white is woven through Loop #4, around #3, through #2, and around #1 of the red. Loop #2 of the white is woven around Loop #4, through #3 of the red, etc. Following the same pattern, complete the weaving. When completed, the heart forms a basket-like container (*see* Diagram D).

6. Cut a handle of whatever color, proportions, and pattern you find pleasing. Staple the handle into the valleys of the heart. This can be done so that the staples will not show.

In Denmark, the basket-weave hearts are filled with small candies and hung, as ornaments, from Christmas trees.

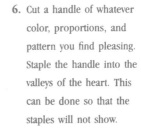

---

*If children are involved, use snub-nosed scissors.

Christmas Garlands

In Denmark, garlands are used to decorate Christmas trees and also as room decorations.

Heart Garland

Materials

- construction paper (12 inch by 12 inch)
- scissors*
- tracing paper *or* bond typing paper
- glue *or* stapler

Instructions

1. From the 12-inch by 12-inch construction paper, cut four 3-inch wide lengths.

2. Fold the lengths of paper into four equal parts. Each part should be 3 inches by 3 inches.

3. Using tracing paper or bond typing paper, trace the pattern at right. Cut out the silhouette of the heart and upper border.

4. Place the silhouette on the top of the folded length of paper and trace the heart onto the folded paper.

5. Cut out the silhouette through the four folds. When the folded paper is unfolded, there should be two hearts hanging from a border. Repeat this process with the other folded lengths of paper.

6. With either glue or a stapler, join the cutouts together to form a garland. Repeat the process to make as long a garland as you wish.

Fold in half

Fold in half again

3″

12″

3″

3″

3″

3″

Pattern

*If children are involved, use snub-nosed scissors.

Dannebrog (Danish Flag) Garland

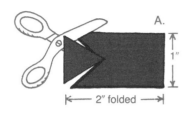

Materials

- construction paper, red
- adhesive tape, white (This tape should be as thin as available.)
- scissors*
- string
- glue

Instructions

1. Cut rectangles 1 inch by 4 inches from the red construction paper.

2. Fold the rectangles in half.

3. Opposite the fold, cut triangles from the ends to form the banner shape illustrated in Diagram A.

4. Using white adhesive tape manufactured for Christmas wrapping, form crosses on both sides of the folded paper (*see* Diagram B). If the only tape available is too wide, cut it in half lengthwise.

5. Fold the flags over the string at regular intervals. Glue the two sides of the flags together (*see* Diagram C).

Three-dimensional Star

Materials

- construction paper or heavy foil paper
- tracing paper or bond typing paper
- scissors*
- straight pins
- ruler
- pencil
- needle and thread

Instructions

1. Using tracing paper or bond typing paper, trace the pattern of the half star, including the interior dots, at the bottom of page 69. Cut out the half star.

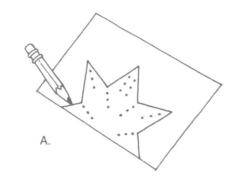

A.

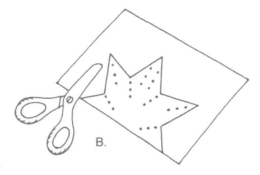

B.

2. Fold a sheet of 12-inch by 12-inch construction paper (or foil) in half. Place the half star silhouette along the fold (*see* Diagram C). Trace the pattern of the half star; with a straight pin, punch holes into the construction paper over the interior dots in the silhouette. Note: It is not really necessary to punch through both halves of the folded paper.

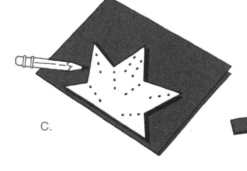

C.

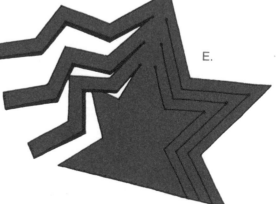

D.

3. With a pencil and ruler, connect the interior holes made in the construction paper (*see* Diagram D). Next, cut out the half star. The fold should run through the center of the full star.

4. Starting at the fold, cut along the penciled lines that connect the pin pricks (*see* Diagram E). Note: You should be cutting through two layers of paper.

E.

---

*If children are involved, use snub-nosed scissors.

68

5. Unfold the star. Note: There should be a connecting "spine" that runs from the top to the bottom of the star. Along this spine are three pairs of "ribs." Beginning with the outer most pair (A), fold the rib on the left back to the spine and crease the paper. Fold the other half in the opposite direction and crease the paper along the "spine." Continue this process for each of the pairs of ribs (B & C). When finished, the star should be "three-dimensional" (*see* Illustration at right above).

6. Perforate the top of the star with a threaded needle and form a loop for hanging.

Pattern

Fold line

Nisse (Danish Christmas Elf)

Materials

- 2 Styrofoam® balls, one somewhat smaller than the other (This craft is designed around a ball 7 inches in circumference and a second ball 6 inches in circumference.)
- construction paper, red and white
- tracing paper or bond typing paper
- toothpick
- short, straight pins with rounded, colored heads (Blue and red are best.)
- acrylic paint, green *or* brown
- paring knife*
- glue
- scissors†

Instructions

1. With a paring knife,* slice off a small section of the larger ball to form a flat bottom. When finished, the ball should sit straight on a tabletop.

2. Paint the larger ball either green or brown.

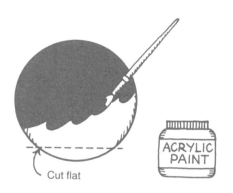

3. Using tracing or typing paper, trace the "collar" and "cap" patterns. Cut out the traced patterns. Outline the patterns on construction paper. The "collar" should be white and the "cap" should be red.

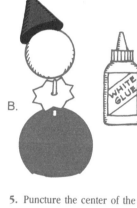

B.

4. Cut the outlines from the construction paper. Place glue along the straight edge of the "cap" and fold it to form a cone (*see* Diagram A).

5. Puncture the center of the "collar" with a toothpick. Center the collar on the toothpick. Connect the two Styrofoam balls with the toothpick (*see* Diagram B).

6. Using a small amount of glue on the inside edge of the "cap," anchor the cap on the elf's head.

7. Stick the pins with colored heads into the Styrofoam ball to make the eyes and a nose on the elf.

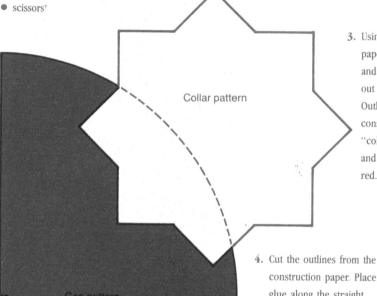

Collar pattern

Cap pattern

Glue here

A.

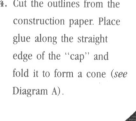

---

*This part of the craft *should not* be attempted without adult supervision.
†If children are involved, use snub-nosed scissors.

Toy Soldier

Materials

- 2 Styrofoam balls, one somewhat smaller than the other (This craft is designed around a ball 7 inches in circumference and a second ball 6 inches in circumference.)
- construction paper, white and red *or* black
- tracing paper or bond typing paper
- toothpick
- short, straight pins with rounded, colored heads (Blue and red are best.)
- red thumb tacks
- acrylic paint, red
- paring knife*   • glue   • scissors†

Instructions

1. With a paring knife,* slice off a small section of the larger ball to form a flat bottom. When finished, the ball should sit straight on a tabletop.

2. Paint the larger of the two balls red.

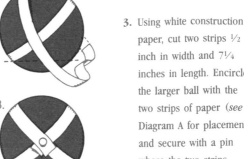

A.

B.

3. Using white construction paper, cut two strips ½ inch in width and 7¼ inches in length. Encircle the larger ball with the two strips of paper (*see* Diagram A for placement) and secure with a pin where the two strips intersect front and back (*see* Diagram B).

4. Using tracing paper or typing paper, trace the "hat" and "plume" patterns at left and below. Cut out the traced patterns. Outline the patterns on construction paper. The plume should be white. The hat should be either red or black.

5. Cut the outlines from the construction paper. Cut slits into the flat edge of the "plume." Fold the "hat" around and glue into place (*see* Diagram C). Glue the plume onto the hat (*see* Diagram D).

6. To make the epaulets use white construction paper. Cut a strip ½ inch in width and 2¼ inches in length. Cut tiny slits into both ends of the strip of paper. Perforate the center of the strip with a toothpick. Center the paper on the toothpick. Connect the two Styrofoam balls with the toothpick. Turn the ends of the strip of paper down to form epaulets (*see* Diagram E).

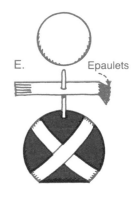

E.   Epaulets

7. Pour a small amount of glue into a lid or cap. Dip the hat into the glue and secure on the soldier's head.

Glue here

Hat pattern

Black

Plume fits here

Plume pattern

Slits

C.

D. Black

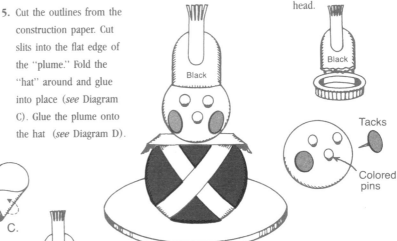

Black

Black

Tacks

Colored pins

8. Using the pins with colored heads, place eyes and a nose on the soldier. Using the red tacks, form red cheeks.

---

*This part of the craft *should not* be attempted without adult supervision.
†If children are involved, use snub-nosed scissors.

71

Christmas Cones

In Denmark, cones are filled with candy and hung, as decorations, from Christmas trees.

Materials

- construction paper or heavy foil
- pencil
- tracing paper or bond typing paper
- scissors*
- glue *or* stapler
- tissue paper, paper doilies, crayons, paint, and other materials for decoration of cones

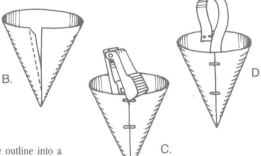

B.

C.

D.

4. Roll the outline into a cone. Using either glue or a stapler, connect the tab side with the other straight side (*see* Diagram B).

5. Cut out a handle and connect it to the cone as shown in Diagram D.

E.

F.

G.

H.

Heart edge

Plain edge

Scallop

Instructions

1. Using tracing paper or typing paper, trace the pattern shown here. The pattern includes three different borders: scallops, a plain edge, and hearts. Choose one.

2. Cut out the fan silhouette. Remember to include the tab along the bottom edge.

3. Place the silhouette on the construction paper (or foil). Outline the silhouette and, then, cut the outline from the sheet of construction paper (*see* Diagram A).

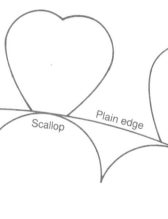

A.

6. Using either paper doilies, tissue paper of various colors, crayons, paints, glitter, stick-on stars and hearts, or whatever materials you choose, decorate the cone. Note the examples E, F, G, and H.

*If children are involved, use snub-nosed scissors.

Tab for gluing

DANISH RECIPES

Ris A L'Amande

(Rice and Almond Pudding)

3¾ cups milk
1 cup long-grain white rice
⅓ cup very fine granulated sugar
½ cup blanched almonds, chopped
½ cup cream sherry
1 tsp. vanilla extract
1 cup whipping cream

(1) Bring the milk to a boil. (2) Add the rice and sugar to the milk. (3) At a lower heat, simmer the rice, uncovered, for 25 minutes. (4) Remove the rice from the heat. When the rice is cool, stir in the almonds, sherry, and vanilla. (5) Whip the cream and fold it into the rice mixture. (6) Turn the pudding into a serving bowl and chill.

Danske Klejner

(Danish Kleiner)

3 eggs
1 cup sugar
4 tbsp. cream
½ cup butter, melted
3-4 cups flour
1 tsp. baking powder
½ tsp. salt
1 tsp. vanilla extract

(1) Cream the eggs and sugar. (2) Add cream and melted butter. (3) Stir in sufficient flour to make a soft but not sticky dough. (4) Add baking powder, salt, and vanilla. (5) Roll dough out to quarter-inch thickness on a lightly floured board. (6) Cut into diamonds about 3 inches long. (7) Slit each diamond in the center. (8) Pass one end of each diamond through the slit. (9) Prepare fat for deep frying. Note: It takes approximately 1½ pounds of lard or vegetable shortening for deep-frying the kleiner. To test the fat for temperature, drop a 1-inch bread cube into it; if the fat is hot enough, the bread cube will brown in 1 minute. (10) Place 6 to 8 diamonds in the hot fat. When the underside is brown, flip the kleiner over in the fat. When both sides are brown, remove the kleiner and allow it to cool on a clean piece of brown wrapping paper. Begin frying the next 6 to 8 kleiners.

Pebbernødder

(Dark Peppernuts)

2 tbsp. lard
2 tbsp. butter
1 cup sugar
1 cup molasses
2 eggs
4 cups flour
¼ tsp. allspice
¼ tsp. cloves
1 tsp. cinnamon

(1) Cream lard, butter, sugar, molasses, and eggs.   (2) Slowly add the flour and spices. (3) Roll the dough into long strips, approximately a half inch in diameter.   (4) Cut the long rolls into half-inch pieces and drop on buttered baking sheets. (5) Bake at 375° F. until cookies are crisp (approximately 10 to 12 minutes).   (6) After cookies have cooled, store in a closed tin.

Rombudding

(Rum Pudding)

1 tbsp. plain gelatin
3 egg yolks
6 tbsp. sugar
2 tbsp. light rum
1 cup whipping cream
1 10 oz. pkg. of frozen raspberries, thawed
1 tbsp. cornstarch

Pudding
(1) Soften gelatin in 3/4 cup of cold water.   (2) Beat egg yolks and sugar in small bowl until thick and lemon-colored. (3) Add the rum.   (4) Dissolve gelatin in pan over boiling water and then cool.   (5) Stir the gelatin into egg mixture. (6) Chill until the gelatin/egg mixture is partially set.   (7) Whip the cream. (8) Fold the whipped cream into the gelatin/egg mixture. (9) Turn into large mold or six individual molds.   (10) Chill until firm.   (11) Unmold and serve with raspberry sauce.

Sauce
(1) Force raspberries through a sieve.   (2) Blend cornstarch with 1/4 cup of water.   (3) Add cornstarch to raspberry juice.   (4) Cook in heavy pan, stiring constantly until mixture is thickened and clear.   (5) Chill before pouring over pudding.

Julekage
(Christmas Coffee Cake)

2 packages compressed yeast
2 cups milk, room temperature
2 eggs, beaten
$\frac{1}{2}$ cup sugar
2 tsp. salt
$\frac{1}{2}$ cup shortening, softened
$7\frac{1}{2}$ cups flour
rind of one lemon, grated
$\frac{1}{4}$ cup citron, chopped
$\frac{1}{2}$ cup blanched almonds, chopped
1 cup raisins
butter

(1) In a large bowl, combine milk with crumbled yeast and stir until the yeast dissolves. (2) Stir in the eggs, sugar, salt, softened shortening, and flour. (3) Knead the dough in the bowl until it is smooth. (4) After greasing the top of the dough, cover the bowl with a cloth. (5) Place bowl in a warm spot for 2 hours. The dough should double in bulk. (6) Punch the dough down into the bowl and work in fruit, nuts, and raisins.

(7) Grease the top of the dough again. (8) Allow dough to stand until it again doubles in size. (9) Drop dough from bowl and divide it into two parts. (10) On a floured board, flatten the two sections of dough into oblongs approximately 1-inch thick. (11) Brush the dough with melted butter. (12) Fold the long edges of the oblongs in toward the center, pressing down well. (13) Move the dough to a greased baking sheet and allow it to rise for a few minutes. (14) In a 350° F. oven, bake for about 45 minutes. (15) Glaze the still warm coffee cake (*see* instructions below).

Glaze
$\frac{1}{2}$ cup confectioners' sugar
$2\frac{1}{2}$ tsp. milk

In a small bowl, mix sugar and milk until smooth. If glaze seems too thick, add extra milk.

Brune Kager
(Brown Christmas Cookies)

1 cup butter or lard
1 cup brown sugar
1 cup dark corn syrup
1 tsp. cardamom
1 tbsp. grated orange peel
1 tsp. cinnamon
1 tsp. cloves
$\frac{1}{2}$ tsp. salt
$\frac{1}{2}$ tsp. allspice
$4\frac{1}{2}$ cups flour
$\frac{1}{4}$ cup finely chopped almonds

(1) At a low heat, melt the butter (lard), sugar, and syrup.
(2) Add the other ingredients and mix well. (3) Form the dough into rolls as if making refrigerator cookies. (4) Store the rolled dough in the refrigerator for 2 to 3 weeks. Aging greatly improves the flavor. (5) Cut the rolls into very thin cookies and decorate each with half of a blanched almond. (6) Bake at 375° F. until the cookies are crisp (approximately 5 to 7 minutes). (7) After cookies have cooled, store in a covered jar or tin.

DANISH CAROLS

LOVELY IS THE DARK BLUE SKY

Nicolai F.S. Grundtvig, 1783–1872 [GKE]

Traditional Danish [WE]

1. Dei - lig er den him - mel blaa, Lyst det er at se der - paa,
1. Love - ly is the dark blue sky, Beau - ti - ful to ev - 'ry eye,

Hvor de gyld - ne stjer - ner blin - ker, Hvor de smi - ler, hvor de vin - ker
Where the gold - en stars are blink - ing, See them smil - ing, see them wink - ing

Os fra jor-den op til sig, Os fra jor-den op til sig.
Beck-'ning us to Heav'n on high, Beck-'ning us to Heav'n on high.

2. *Det var midt i julenat,*
   Hver en stierne glimtet matt;
   Men med ett der blev at skue
   En saa klar paa himlens bue,
   Som en liten stjernesol,
   Som en liten stjernesol.

3. *Østerlands de vise menn*
   Fandt dog stjernen der igjen,
   Some de skuet i det høie;
   Ti i barnets milde øie
   Funklende og klar den sat,
   Funklende og klar den sat.

2. On the earliest Christmas night,
   All the stars were shining bright,
   When, among them, burst in brilliance
   One lone star whose streaming radiance
   Far surpassed the sun's own light,
   Far surpassed the sun's own light.

3. Wise men from the East afar,
   Led to Jesus by the star,
   There adoring Heav'n's elected,
   Found within his eyes reflected
   God's great Light, and Love, and Pow'r.
   God's great Light, and Love, and Pow'r.

CHILD JESUS

Hans Christian Andersen, 1805–1875 [GKE]

Niels Gade, 1817–1890 [WE]

Andante

1. Barn Je - sus i en Kryb - be laa, Skjønt Him - len var hans
1. Child Je - sus in a man - ger lay, Yet Heav - en was His

Ej - e, Hans Pu - de her blev Hø of Straa, Morkt
own.___ His low - ly pil - low was of straw, And

var det om hans Lej - e; Men Stjer - nen o - ver
round Him no light shone;___ But in the sky the

2. Hver sorgfuld Sjael, bliv karsk og glad,
   Ryst af din tunge Smerte,
   Et Barn er født i Davids Stad,
   Til Trøst for hvert et Hjerte;
   Til Barnet vil vi stige ind
   Og blive, Børn i Sjael og Sind.
   Halleluja, Halleluja, Halleluja!

3. O sorrowing soul, be glad today,
   Cast out your bitter pain;
   For Bethle'm's Babe will show the way
   We heav'nly bliss can gain.
   Let us with childlike heart and mind
   Seek now the Son of God to find.
   Alleluia, Alleluia, Alleluia!

Acknowledgments

Cover:	Bo Bedre, Lavinia Press	29:	Soren Rud, Alfa Foto
2:	Christian Lorentz, Politikens Pressefoto	30:	Lennard
		31:	Politikens Pressefoto
6:	Lennard	32:	Alfa Foto
7:	Lennard	33:	Soren Rud, Alfa Foto
9:	Politikens Pressefoto	35:	Erik Betting, A/S Pressehuset
10:	(Top) Soren Rud, Alfa Foto (Bottom) Sisse Brimberg from Lennard	36:	Erik Betting, A/S Pressehuset
		37:	Alfa Foto
11:	Nina Lemvigh-Müller/Alfa Foto	38:	Sisse Brimberg, Woodfin Camp Inc.
12:	Lennard	39:	Willi Hansen, Alfa Foto
13:	Peer Pedersen, Politikens Pressefoto	40:	Lennard
14:	Gunnar Pedersen, A/S Pressehuset	41:	(Top) Soren Madsen, Alfa Foto (Bottom) Alfa Foto
15:	Sisse Brimberg, Woodfin Camp Inc.	43:	Lennard
16:	(Top) Bo Jarner, A/S Pressehuset (Bottom) Lennard	44:	Soren Rud, Alfa Foto
		45:	Lars Poulsen, Politikens Pressefoto
17:	World Book photo	46:	Soren Rud, Alfa Foto
18:	World Book photo	47:	Busser, Politikens Pressefoto
19:	Lavinia Press	48:	Politikens Pressefoto
20:	Lennard	49:	Soren Rud, Alfa Foto
21:	Lavinia Press	50:	Kai Honkanen
22:	A/S Pressehuset	51:	Sisse Brimberg, Woodfin Camp Inc.
23:	(Top) Erik Betting, A/S Pressehuset (Bottom) Politikens Pressefoto	52:	Sisse Brimberg, Woodfin Camp Inc.
		53:	Sisse Brimberg, Woodfin Camp Inc.
24:	Lavinia Press	54:	Sisse Brimberg, Woodfin Camp Inc.
25:	Lennard	55:	Sisse Brimberg, Woodfin Camp Inc.
26:	Lennard	64:	Lavinia Press
27:	Alfa Foto		
28:	Lennard		